Your Health is *Your* Greatest Wealth

Your Journey to a Vibrant, Healthy Mind and Body

Raewyn Weller

Your Health is Your Greatest Wealth: Your Journey to a Vibrant, Healthy Mind and Body: © Raewyn Weller 2020

raewynweller.com

The moral rights of Raewyn Weller to be identified as the author of this work have been asserted in accordance with the New Zealand **Copyright** Act 1994

First published in Australia 2020 by Gowor International Publishing

ISBN: 978-0-6488067-3-8

Any opinions expressed in this work are exclusively those of the author and are not necessarily the views held or endorsed by Gowor International Publishing

Any part of this publication may be reproduced or transmitted by any means, electronic, photocopying or otherwise, without prior written permission of the author.

Disclaimer

The author of this book does not dispense medical advice or prescribe the use of any technique as a form of treatment for physical, emotional, or medical problems either directly or indirectly. The intent of the author is only to offer information, inspiration and edutainment to help you in your quest for emotional, physical and spiritual well-being, and to offer a variety of information to provide a wide range of choices recognising that we all have widely diverse circumstances and viewpoints. Should any reader choose to make use of the information herein, that is their constitutional right and decision. The author and publisher do not assume any responsibilities whatsoever for the personal or other success, results, action or fulfilment upon the readers' decision to use this information.

Foreword

Your Health is Your Greatest Wealth is an inspiring book.

In its pages, Raewyn reveals decades of experience and knowledge on how to maximise our wellbeing and squeeze every drop of meaning and fulfilment from the life we live.

Her deep understanding of the inextricable relationship between the mind, body, and all other aspects of our lives will empower you, as she shares practical ideas and profound wisdom on how to reach new levels of energy and vitality.

The knowledge she shares in this book will benefit you in every way, every day of your life.

Having known Raewyn for many years, I can say with a hand on my heart that this extraordinary woman not only knows her topic inside and out, but that she cares about people's wellbeing on the deepest level. Her mission in this world is undoubtedly a critical one, especially with the growing levels of stress and dis-ease modern humanity is experiencing.

I am thankful for her reminder in my own journey to look after what is undoubtedly my greatest wealth, too: my health.

This book truly is an encyclopaedia of wisdom. Read it thoroughly and use it daily to support yourself in rediscovering your inner spark and living the vibrant life that you deserve.

With inspiration,

Emily Gowor

Dedication and Acknowledgements

Your Health is Your Greatest Wealth is dedicated to my clients, friends, family and you the reader and healer. Yes, that means you, because *you* are a healer.

A big thank you to everyone that has entered my life and to all of my life experiences, the good, the bad and the ugly; you have all taught me many lessons, enabling me to adjust my course when needed and move on.

Thank you to my family, friends, work colleagues and staff that I have observed over the years and my many clients in more recent years.

And most of all a BIG thank you to the great masters of healthy thinking, living, energy healing, and personal development, that I have learnt from. I am so grateful to you all. Thank you, thank you ☺

To my partner Gus for his patience and suggestions, to my friend Rhonda, thank you for the many hours of sitting, reading, reviewing and making great suggestions with my manuscript in the final stages. And an even bigger thanks you to my editor Andrew Jackson. I have always said, "I am a graduate of the school of life, that I went to school to eat my lunch," hence often my grammar, spelling and punctuation have quite some room for improvement, I am a very creative speller; English was never a great past time for me at school.

Thank you to my granddaughters Courtney and Elesha, and the many people from all walks of life for your suggestions and creative intelligence towards the cover, believe me it changed many times.

If I can do it, so can you. I am sure you have a book within you, don't die with that book still in you, especially if it can help others.

This leads me to Emily Gowor;

Thank you, Emily, for your great advice and guidance throughout my journey, I am sure you were frustrated with me at times ☺.

If you have a book in you, I recommend you talk to Emily, her contacts are in the back of this book.

"Life changes in a moment, 'When you make a decision'"

Preface

"Great spirits have always encountered violent opposition from Mediocre minds"'

A midwinter's day, June 2018 in Mount Maunganui New Zealand. The sun was shining, the birds were flitting to and fro, singing in the trees and a soft warm breeze whisked across me. 'What an atmosphere,' I thought, as I sat outside in the sun sorting a pile of papers, many full of wisdom from wise souls that had attracted me over the years. I had been collecting notes for the past 12 to 15 years, now it was decision time. What to keep and share with you in this book and what to discard.

Wow-what a fantastic journey my life has been. I am blessed with so much inner peace, happiness and good health, feeling gratitude for my busy fulfilled life, which appears a short life thus far. With love in my heart, I am excited to share with you, all of the lessons I have learnt and the wisdom I have gained, so please read on and enjoy.

There is a great deal of information and many exercises in this book; don't feel that you have to take it all in at once. Please use it as a reference book. I have many reference books in my library that I refer to frequently, some I just pick up and open at a page and find that the information in front of me is relevant to what is happening in my life. It is a lesson to take heed of in the moment, others I reread and learn more from each time I do so.

I am a learning junkie and I hope that will continue as it keeps my brain alert. I have always said that I went to school to eat my lunch and haven't stopped learning since I left. I will continue to seek new tools, modalities, and information that will expand my life. At the same time enabling me to help others, anyone willing to read, listen, learn and heal, as I share my knowledge and skills.

I have always had a hunger to share and help others to help themselves, whatever I have pursued in life, there has always been an urge to help others grow and improve their lives. When I started on the journey of writing 'Your Health is Your Greatest Wealth', the intention was to share all of the wonderful knowledge and skills I had gained over the many years of learning that would help you, the reader, on a journey to a happier, more vibrant and healthy life. I had no idea just how momentous it would be and how much I would learn and grow on that journey.

I had so much information and so many tools to share within me, jotted on paper from seminars and online learning, also on my computer. It all needed to be sorted and I wasn't quite sure of which direction it would take me. It has taken almost two years to write, and while doing so, I continued to learn new skills and information. It became bigger than I ever had imagined. It really boggled my mind. What do I include? Where do I start or more to the point, stop?

I took a break after about 15 months, sat back for a while, then came back to it and wow, I realised how powerful the information I was sharing was. In no way am I claiming all of this knowledge as mine, I have ridden on the backs of many amazing healers, authors and health experts; too many to mention. My apologies to any of these amazing people if I have quoted something you may have said or taught me that I have not acknowledged you for. I may have often just learnt and started using amazing tools, sayings and information over the years, and often forgotten exactly where it came from. When we give, we always receive and learn even more. I am continually learning, whether it is from the books and videos I watch, study and practice, from the mistakes I make, or the people I encounter in everyday life. I love it.

In this book, I am sharing information, tools, techniques, and simple exercises to enable you to help yourself towards healing your mind, body, and spirit that all lead to healthy living if used. To help you discover how your actions, reactions, thoughts, beliefs, past experiences, plus more could be imprisoning you, holding you back, possibly in pain, causing disease within your mind, body, and spirit. Learn how to turn your health, relationships, and life around, how to free, love and heal yourself.

I envisage 'Your Health is Your Greatest Wealth' helping so many, but it will only happen if you take on board the information I am sharing with you and take the appropriate action. Each time I read through what I have written, I remember a tool I haven't used myself for a while and again expand my thinking and knowledge. I hope that it comes to be one of the most used books in your library. Please read it, highlight what resonates with you, and use it as a reference book and a tool to live your greatest life. Read, rinse and repeat. Read, take action, repeat.

Anyone who has met and really got to know me, knows how enthusiastic I am about life and helping others. My mission in life is to share my knowledge, energise and inspire people to help themselves. This book is the manifestation of my purpose in life, which is to help as many people as possible understand how to strive for and live a greater, healthier life, feeling fulfilled. I take great pleasure in sharing my knowledge, hoping to inspire everyone who reads this book to live an amazing, happy, healthy, disease-free life.

My family and friends have heard me say that I am writing a book for almost two years. Hey, we all know that Rome wasn't built in a day. Yahoo, it is here, in the palm of your hands and just look at the resources that are there to help you move forward, enabling you to create a fantastic life. I have enjoyed this journey and wish you an amazing one in return, to a better life, full of vitality. And I know it won't be for everyone, we are all different and have our own journey.

But for those who are ready and willing, *Your Health is Your Greatest Wealth* is not just a book; it is part of me. You will feel my energy, my presence in these pages. As you embark on the journey of reading this book, it is my genuine wish that I have achieved my mission and that, by the time you turn the last page, you will have the tools to help yourself, be inspired to take action and without too much effort, maintain a healthy life, your greatest wealth.

Thank you so much, in purchasing this book. You have invested in your life.

I love you.

Aroha Raewyn

PS This is a get out of prison free card – free yourself of pain, depression, negative thoughts, disease of your mind, body, and spirit.

Content

Foreword v

Dedication and Acknowledgements vii

Preface ix

Introduction 1

PART 1 The Power of Your Mind 9

Chapter 1: Understanding the Power of Your Mind 10

    Everything first begins in the mind 11
    Your mind is the most amazing power tool 13
    Monitor your thinking 16
    There's no drug more powerful 19

Chapter 2: Conscious v's Subconscious Mind 23

    The three levels of your mind 24
    Your thoughts create your reality 27
    You can change the channel 30
    Your Inherent mental power 33
    We all have choices 38

Chapter 3: You Become What You Think About 44

    Your mind does what it thinks you want 45
    Your happiness chemicals 49
    Thoughts affect your health 54
    Medical histories are like peering into a crystal ball 58

Chapter 4: Your Mind Loves Familiarity and Habits 62

    Repetition forms familiarity and habits 63
    What is a habit? 65

Change your habits, change your life 70
Fear 75

Chapter 5: Nothing Happens by Mistake, We Are Not Broken 79
Your body can heal itself.. 80
Dis-ease must have a cause... 84
Nothing can irritate you without your consent......................... 87
Your most destructive critic is you 90

PART 2 Solutions for Healthy Living.. 92

Take Control of Your Power, Your Life.. 93
Are you reliving the past?.. 94
Forgiveness and letting go... 97
Healthy thinking is paramount 102
Emotions and feelings 108
The rise and fall of thoughts.. 112
Thoughts with feelings strengthen the outcome.................... 115

Self-Esteem 118
What you think about yourself does matter 119
Set up a self-esteem Bank 126
Empowering from within... 128
Self-help exercise to improve your self-esteem 132

Control Your Stress, Change Your Life...................................... 138
What is Stress? 139
Reduce Stress – Declutter.. 144
Laughter can cure 147
Take Control of your Thoughts 149

Food – Good or Bad? 152
Food is energy.. 153
Are you eating intelligently?.. 157

We have worldwide epidemics	161
Sugar – How bad and why	162
My take on Fats and Oils	167

Life Force Energy 173

Energy and your chakras	174
Fresh air and nature	187
Sunshine	189
The benefits of water	192
Exercise mind and body	198
Colour your life	202
Crystals	205
Toxins in your life	208

Relationships 213

What happens after the honeymoon?	214
Know your love language	216
Choose your friends wisely	218
Loneliness is a major issue	221

Music and Meditation 223

The benefits of music	224
Heal with meditation	228
Take time to relax	233

Sleep 235

The Importance of quality sleep	236
Tips to help you sleep better	240

Muscle Testing 244

What is muscle testing?	245
Can I muscle-test myself?	247
Using a pendulum	249

Exercises and Remedies 252
    Daily routine to energise your mind and body 253
    Healing ball exercise 265
    Self-healing exercise 267
    Benefits of reflexology and other energy moving techniques ... 268
    Probable causes for common ailments 272
    Life's Lessons to consider 278
    Positive ways to deal with negative feelings 281
    Thought-provoking questions 283
    Boost your health and vitality 285
    Reprogram your subconscious mind 288
    Protecting and clearing yourself from unwanted energies 290
    Wheel of Life 297

A Real-Life Story to Conclude with 298

Conclusion 302

Recommended Websites and Reading 306

About the Author 310

Introduction

Your Health is Everything

Your body is just the place that your memory calls home.

"Deepak Chopra"

Are you seeking a smoother road to travel in life? Do you want a life full of vitality and good health? Yes? Well you are on the right road by reading this book.

We all have our own journey; I am a firm believer that everything in your life happens for a reason and most of the time that reason is you, your thoughts, choices and actions. There is a reason you picked this book to read, because you are searching for answers.

Have you ever noticed that every time something happens to you, you are there?

There are no mistakes, only learning curves. I will show you how you create your own life, whether you believe it or not, you have attracted everything you have received and the experiences you have encountered, whether you perceive them as good, bad or indifferent. They are there for you to learn and grow from.

We meet the people we are meant to meet; I am sure you have heard the old saying "People come into your life for a reason, a season or a lifetime."

Life is a rollercoaster to be enjoyed; you are on this planet for a reason, to serve a purpose, some for a short time, others a long time. Each of us has chosen to be here, some say we even chose our parents, many find this debatable. We all have our own journey to undertake. The great news is "you are not stuck with your current life; if you are not happy, you can change it."

There is so much you can do to promote good health and happiness in your mind, body and life which I cover in this book.

As the late New Zealand Doctor (Surgeon turned naturopath) Ulric Williams said:

"You don't have to do anything to get better; all you need is to stop doing what's wrong and making you sick."

I have always thought outside of the square and have challenged myself and others in doing so. Coming from NZ, I am determined not to be just another sheep that follows the crowd; hence why I have been down many different roads, taking the path that is less used and I don't just agree with others. I can be a little provocative at times, but respect others' opinions, even if I don't agree. *Live and let live* is the name of the game.

We all have choices, so, instead of being a sheep, I have decided to be a BULL. Just like a bull, I often charge in and just do it. Sometimes I am right and sometimes wrong; life is a learning curve, a rollercoaster with ups and downs. By being a bull, I believe I have become 'Able' as I am sure you are too –Love-able, Cap-able, Answer-able, Account-able, Predict-able, or in my case, maybe Unpredict-able, Response-able, Reason-able, Accept-able, Touch-able, Hug-able, Incred-able, Adapt-able, Respect-able, Depend-able, Rely-able, Afford-able, Value-able and most importantly, Cure-able.

Introduction

As you can see, I have a sense of humour which is needed to live a healthy happy life. When you smile and laugh, endorphins, happy hormones, are released into your bloodstream, which promotes a sense of relaxation and wellbeing.

You will notice that throughout the book I refer to 'disease' as 'dis-ease', simply because I believe that is what it is, dis-ease of the mind and body, it is your body telling you there is something wrong.

We reap what we sow! This book is a journey to teach you how to plant good seeds in that magnificent mind of yours, to nurture them and reap the benefits. Yes, we *do* reap what we sow; we do create our life, which may come as a shock to some.

With *'Your Health is your Greatest Wealth'*, I want to take you on a journey to enable you to move forward. Taking you from pain to pleasure, unhappy to happy, from anger, resentments, jealousy, envy, whatever it is inside of you disturbing your health and peace of mind, to having love for yourself, full of joy, contentment, gratitude and living a vibrant, healthy life.

However, before you can move on, you first need to see where you are now, to know what needs fixing, where you are starting from. What areas of your life are causing you pain or dis-ease, either mentally, physically or emotionally? How balanced or to the contrary, out of balance are you?

I encourage you to do the exercise below now.

Join the lines in each section on the 'Wheel of Life' to see how balanced you are.

0 being not good, 10 being great.

Wheel Of Life

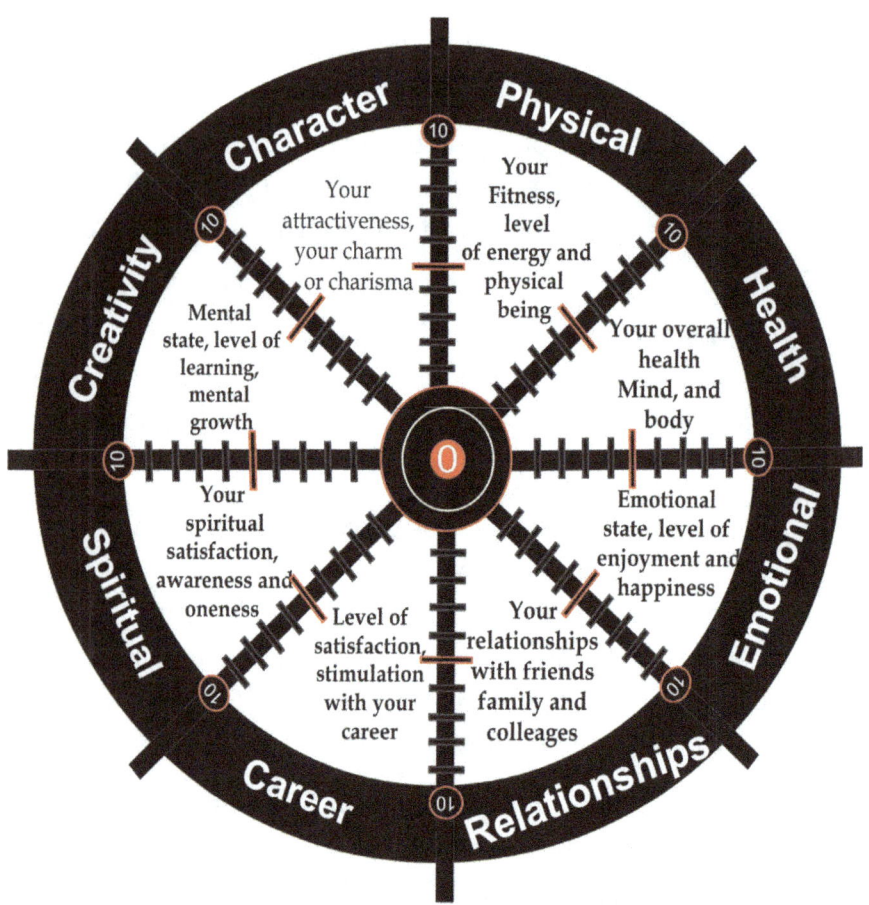

Are you travelling a rocky road? Do you have a flat tyre? Now you know what areas you need to work on. ☺

Without a balanced life and good health, your life is limited.

When you have completed the book, having undertaken the exercises and suggestions I recommend, and taken on board the appropriate information for you, I encourage you to also complete the 'Wheel of Life' at the back of the book.

Hopefully you will see a great improvement, a much more balanced wheel.

Just as every house needs stable, well balanced foundations and every mighty tree has solid roots to stand tall and hold its ground, you need to be stable and grounded with a balanced mind, body and spirit. If there are termites (past hurts, events, issues, worry and stress) eating at your foundations, then above (your body and mind) will be affected and possibly cave in causing dis-ease. No mighty oak, or house will stay standing if its foundations are eaten away by termites.

You are the architect of your life, the captain of your ship and must take control, so a strong wind or storm in your life doesn't blow you off course. So, pump up that flat tyre.

I am a big believer that you need to put yourself first (I didn't always believe or do that), be selfish, but in a good way. You need to love the person you are, so that you can share your love, wisdom and energy with others. When you give, you receive.

The intention of *'Your Health is Your Greatest Wealth'* is to give you knowledge and tools to help transform your internal software (your thoughts), which will transform your external life. I will give you the seeds and if you allow, plant them in your mind. You need to learn how to nurture them and grow your magnificent mind, body and life.

I have followed and learnt from many amazing people and books on different subjects and fields of healing, dis-ease, personal development and business over many years.

The biggest lesson I have learnt on this journey is – 'that everything I need is within me'. Too often we look outside of ourselves for all of the answers.

My second lesson is – 'I need to receive as well as give, to believe in, look after and love myself so I have the right energy to share, help and teach others that are willing to learn how to improve their life'.

I have included references and recommendations of books to read and people to study in the back of the book. There are so many brilliant people out there to learn from: Not just from 'gurus', but everyday people you meet, like family and friends, from young children to 100-year-olds. Everyone has something to teach us and if you look for the positive in everyone and everything that happens to cross your path, you will benefit immensely. I always say 'if you aren't learning, you are not living and the first person to learn is yourself'. Learn from your mistakes, from everything and everyone you encounter in life.

Are you getting forgetful, stressed, depressed, have low self-esteem, or aches and pains? Men, are you feeling like a failure in bed, getting that podgy tummy? Then check out the chapter on Self-esteem and maybe the food. Oh gosh, I think you need to read the whole book. It's scary, I know, as one ailment turns into another.

Given the right knowledge, mindset and with persistence, you CAN turn these issues around. Your body can heal itself, given the right conditions. Life is to be lived, not in pain and misery, with memory loss, body failing, falling apart, in discomfort and the dis-ease that many people live with, but with vibrancy, joy, feeling happy, bright, fit and healthy. Grow old gracefully.

You are a healer; we are all healers. I am totally convinced that everyone can heal themselves, given the right state of mind (healthy thinking). There are so many people out there that have cured themselves of cancer, diabetes, addictions, joint pain plus much more without drugs and surgery. They just changed their mindset, their attitude and lifestyle. Where your mind goes, energy flows and vice-versa, so we need to think how we are thinking.

A few people that I admire and have learnt from that have cured themselves are:- Dr Fredrick Bailes, who cured himself of Diabetes before insulin had been discovered; Louise Hayes who cured herself of cancer; Chunyi Li Master of Spring forest Qi Gong cured himself of arthritis and severe suicidal depression; and 'Energy Medicine Lady,' Donna Eden who healed herself of multiple sclerosis.

Modern research is so amazing; it shows that we can turn our brain and almost all dis-ease around; your body CAN heal itself. Within a year, almost every cell in your body, if not all of them have renewed. You are not stuck with the life you have; you can change it. You just need to know how and take that leap of faith in yourself.

I have not had any major ailments, but without drugs or surgery, have turned painful grinding hips around; cured oncoming headaches and sore throats in minutes, anger and self-esteem into forgiveness, having to deal with sexual encounters in my younger days. At one stage in life, I regularly sprained my ankles. I changed that with the mindset to having strong ankles. I used to have regular colds, now I seldom have them. We just need to think how we are thinking at the time of discomfort and learn where our dis-ease is coming from. Look after ourselves to turn it around, feed our mind and body the right food. It works; our bodies are designed to heal themselves.

My gift to you is the offer of suggestions, guidance, tools and exercises. To hopefully excite and inspire you enough to want to take action and make better choices that will turn your life around, feeling rejuvenated, enthusiastic, happy and healthy.

You don't have to believe, but it helps. You have a magnificent mind and body; know it, believe it, love it, and love yourself. When you are fit and healthy and love yourself, you then, and only then, have the energy to fully love and help others.

Life is like a mirror; it reflects back what you put out.

Allow me to help you make Vitality and Healthy Living Your Reality, enjoy the journey.

Live Love and Laugh with Good Health and Energy

Aroha, Raewyn

*"When life gives you a hundred reasons to cry,
Show life you have a thousand reasons to smile."
"Turn the Lemon into Lemonade".*

Part 1

The Power of Your Mind

Chapters

Understanding the Power of Your MIND 10
Conscious V's Subconscious Mind 23
You Become What You Think About 44
Your Mind Loves Familiarity and Habits 62
Nothing Happens by Mistake, We Are Not Broken 79

Chapter 1
Understanding the Power of Your MIND

Everything first begins in the mind.. 11
Your mind is the most amazing power tool 13
Monitor your thinking 16
There's no drug more powerful.. 19

"Creation is always happening. Every time an individual has a thought, or a prolonged, chronic way of thinking, they're in the creation process. Something is going to manifest out of those thoughts."

Michael Beckwith - Agape Church Los Angeles

Everything begins first in the mind

Think about it. The chair you are sitting on, the glasses you may be wearing, a table, picture, your car, the great pyramids and Eiffel Tower, every one of these were created in somebody's mind before it manifested into form. Even the meals you eat, someone thought of what to buy and cook before preparing the meal.

Likewise, the words you say to yourself and the pictures you create in your mind, create your life.

Your mind is a gold mine, it is your most valuable asset, you need to look after it, feed it well; quality is paramount when investing in it.

Understanding is powerful; your mind is the most powerful thing that you have control of. If you don't control it, it will control you. Even though it is hard to believe at times, when you do finally grasp the fact and fully understand how amazingly powerful your mind is, you will know how you can and do create your life. With this knowledge, if you think positive thoughts and take the right action, you will transform your life.

Did you fill in the Wheel of Life to determine where you are at and what you need to work on? If not, please go back and do it. If your life, (your wheel) is unbalanced, you will be travelling a rocky road. If you are unbalanced emotionally, physically, mentally or energetically, your whole world will be breaking into chaos. You can, with the right self-care re-balance your health, energy, relationships and life. When you learn to take note of and take responsibility for what's happening in your life, you can adjust your course and have an amazing life. You can get off your rocky road onto a tar sealed road; it makes for a smoother ride.

You have the power, the means, and *with will*, you can mend your body. Your body works and heals itself subconsciously, given the right conditions; with your conscious guidance it will do a better job. We were all born with a wonderful mind/body connection. Your MIND is the key to healing your body. Everything in your body can heal itself, except your teeth.

Most of your body is controlled by your subconscious mind, you don't have to tell your heart how to pump blood around your entire body, your lungs how to breathe, your lymphatic system to cleanse your body fluids, your kidneys, liver or any organ how to do its job. You can cut or burn yourself and your skin will automatically heal itself. So, if you look after your mind and body, exercise it, feed it, rest it and water it well and keep a positive mind, your body will look after you. Your subconscious mind is pre-programmed, the biggest problem of which is, we don't come with a user's manual and there are definitely no delete buttons.

Most people look after their cars, phones and computers better than their body. If you put kerosene in your car, do you expect it to go? How can you expect your body to work well for you if you don't look after it by feeding it the right food and regularly servicing it well? And just importantly your mind needs regular care, exercise and good thoughts. We need to do a check-up from the neck up often, to think how we are thinking.

Are you looking after your mind and body? Within this book, I will give you tips and exercises to help you on the right path to a vibrant, healthy mind and body, should you choose to take it.

"The mind of man is capable of anything."

'Joseph Conrad'

Your mind is the most amazing power tool you have

Just know and believe that you have a magnificent MIND and that you can take control of it.

Technology is advancing at such a phenomenal rate that developers are squeezing computer components into smaller and smaller spaces, so much so that it is possible to fit millions of microprocessors onto the head of a pin. Yet despite this rapid growth in capacity, the human brain remains the most powerful "computer" on the Planet. If you could look inside your brain, you would find it contained 100 Billion nerve cells called neurons. Each of these has the equivalent of around 60 Megabytes of RAM, that's enough to process thousands of operations every second. Multiply that by 100 Billion and you will get some idea of the power sitting on top of your shoulders. This is kind of mind boggling for people like me in their senior years.

I have loved learning and changing the neural pathways in my brain. I have found it so fascinating and just want to keep sharing what I am continually learning. The brain is so amazing, through what is called neuroplasticity or brain plasticity. It can form and reorganize synaptic connections, forming new neural pathways, and is continually changing, especially in response to learning and new experiences.

Neuroplasticity allows our neurons (nerve cells) in the brain to compensate for injury and dis-ease and to adjust their activities in response to new learning, situations, experiences and environmental change.

Neural pathways are like superhighways of nerve cells that transmit messages. Every time you do or learn something new, you create a neural pathway; there is a connection between two neurons which is called a synaptic connection. It is widely accepted that the synapse plays a role in the formation of your memory, every time you repeat the same thing, the connection becomes stronger and you are forming a habit.

The process of neuroplasticity is present throughout your lifespan and involves many different processes. As mentioned, it involves creating new neural pathways or connections as well as "synaptic pruning" which is getting rid of old connections that are no longer necessary or useful.

Neuroplasticity plays a role in everything from learning a new language to healing after a stroke, even in habitual emotional states. For example, people suffering from depression are literally "wired" for feeling sad and hopeless—but the good news is, the laws of neuroplasticity tell us this wiring can be changed. Wow, this tells me we need to stay positive, and keep learning new things, good things.

Research in the latter half of the 20th century has shown that many aspects of the brain can be altered throughout our whole life. The developing brain of children has a higher degree of plasticity than the adult brain, hence as we get older, we need to keep doing and learning new things to keep our magnificent brain active and replace old neuro pathways with new better ones that serve us. With the proper mindset and intention, along with the proper nourishment and stimulation, the brain can heal, grow, and adapt at any stage of life.

This brings to mind the old saying "use it or lose it".

I have followed Dr. Daniel Amen MD of the 'Amen Clinic' in the US for many years and simply love the work he does. He has some great sayings and here is one to ponder on, "You are not stuck with the brain you have" meaning if you change your thinking, and avoid toxic environments, you can change your life. With the research he and many other brain specialists and neuroscientist's have conducted over the last few decades, we are being shown that the neuroplasticity of the brain is forever changing. When you change your brain, you change your life. Imagine how drug addicts are changing their lives, eek.

Just like a computer, we were born with a blank canvas and as we grow up, our brain becomes programmed. Throughout our childhood, we are learning new things, taking in information through all of our senses; see, hear, smell, taste and touch. We are programmed by our parents, teachers, peers, siblings, our actions and the experiences and events in our life from the day we are born, creating neural pathways, forming habits and programs within.

We expand on the forming and changing of habits in chapter 4.

But guess what? As an adult, you can do your own programming, or should I say *reprogramming*. With conscious effort, you can change what is already programmed into your brain. I am not saying it is easy, but with will power and persistence, you can do it. Even though we are continuously bombarded with information from all angles, at home, work, school, through the news and social media, we have choices. We need to monitor what we are taking onboard, choosing to believe, and/or allowing to upset us.

You can change the channels just like on your TV or radio if you don't like the program you are watching or hearing.

> "The mind is its own place and in itself,
> Can make a Heaven of Hell, a Hell of Heaven."
> 'John Milton'

Monitor your thinking

When you learn to take note of and take responsibility for what's happening in your life, you can adjust your course and have an amazing life. You can get off your rocky road onto a tar sealed road; it makes for a much smoother ride.

Earlier, I referred to 'doing a regular check-up from the neck up'. In other words, take note and be conscious of what you're thinking, what is going on in your mind and what regularly comes out of your mouth like the words you use. When you make a point of being consciously aware of your thoughts and words you use, you will see a pattern in your thinking.

The good news is, we can change neural pathways that have been formed at any time. You can forge new pathways within, creating new thinking, attitudes and habits. When you become aware of your thinking, you notice patterns, some positive and some negative. Being aware of your thoughts is the first step. Once you are aware of what you are thinking and saying to yourself continuously, you can make changes; you can stop yourself if negative or praise yourself if positive. What you keep repeating will be your reality.

I can just hear you saying 'hey Raewyn, that's easier said than done. How?'

To do a regular check up from the neck up, monitor your thinking. Take a note pad and for a whole day, or maybe a week, write it down every time you find yourself saying or thinking something negative, like if you swear, write it down. You will find that if you swear a lot, you will be angry inside, at someone or something. People who are content with themselves, are happy people and don't normally swear, that is unless they have formed a habit of swearing.

Another of Dr Amen's sayings is *'you need to eradicate your 'ANT's'* short for 'Automatic Negative Thoughts' and 'Ant Eaters' being the solution to eradicate automatic negative thoughts. We have these ANT's at all ages, and they can keep repeating themselves, if not kept in check. Negative thoughts affect your brain and your life, it is best to eradicate them. Too many ANT's can and will form bad habits; we need to change them to APTAA's (Automatic Positive Thoughts and Actions).

Remember Henry Ford's saying "**If you think you can or think you can't, you're right**." We all have choices and our choices create our life. Always remember – "the words you say to yourselves and others, and the pictures you create in your head, create your reality". I will repeat these words regularly because they are so important and repetition is how you learn. If there is one thing I want you to get from this book, it is 'Repetition forms a habit and it is so important to check your thinking and words regularly. So form a habit of monitoring your thinking regularly.' If you want to change your reality, you need to start with your thoughts and words. Choose to think and act positively, learn continually, learn from all encounters, experiences and people and turn negative experiences into learning curves.

Another quote from Henry Ford:

"Failure is simply the opportunity to begin again, this time more intelligently."

Everything happens for a reason, learn from it.

It's not always what you do or say, it is often how you do or say things that make the difference. If you put your heart and energy into anything, it will work. If you make a mistake, learn from it, just as inventor Thomas Edison made 1,000 unsuccessful attempts at inventing the light bulb. When a reporter asked, "How did it feel to fail 1,000 times?" Edison replied, "I didn't fail 1,000 times. The light bulb was an invention with 1,000 steps."

Constantly do new things, challenge yourself and frequently think how you are thinking and eventually, you *will* change your life.

"You have power over your mind – not outside events. Realise this, and you will find strength."

'Marcus Aurelius'

"There's no drug more powerful"

I have found this all so fascinating and exciting, learning really is a game. It took me many years to learn that I was not stuck with my current way of life and thinking. Learning about the plasticity of our brain and the neural pathways we create in it, knowing that our brain can and is continually changing as we learn and do new things, was so exciting for me. We can turn our life around by changing our thinking and I have done that several times over the last decade or two. Yes, I started working on myself late. Believe me, it is never too late.

In the past, we were taught that if the brain has been damaged, there is as little to no hope, and so many believe that if they have a genetic gene that has been passed down from generation to generation, it is inevitable that they too will get it. Those days are gone. Knowing that you have a tendency towards a genetic condition is now just a warning bell to say 'if you don't change your thinking and do something about it and you think you will, you will most likely get it. But you don't have to, you can change your brain; you can change your health and your life'.

My life would be doomed if I believed that if certain Dis-eases were genetic because it has affected someone in my family, I would get it. My father passed away in his mid-60s with pancreatic cancer. Heart problems took many of his family, my mother lost a breast to cancer in her 60's; she has undergone 20-plus operations for different things in her lifetime, Alzheimer's started setting in when she was in her mid-80s and she had a stroke at 88. My sister was a type-one diabetic from the age of 10, losing both legs (several operations), several fingers, her eyesight, kidneys and she passed away at the age of 52 with gangrene in the base of her spine.

I have never broken a bone, I did crack one once; have never had an operation or had any major illness, and I am very fit and healthy at the age of 70. I have no intention of letting my health slip and will stay happy with 'who I am' for many years to come.

I had a birthday card given to me a few years ago which read;

Life is not a journey to the grave with the intention of arriving safely in a well-preserved body, but rather a skid in broadside, thoroughly used up, totally worn out and loudly proclaiming WHOA – WHAT A RIDE.

I framed it, as that is how I thought then, I now think before I leap.

I still intend to have a great journey, but not totally worn out. I now look after my mind and body. I exercise both mind and body through walking, cycling, swimming in the surf, I enjoy badminton and table tennis occasionally, and dancing a lot -mainly Rock n' Roll. I also practice Qigong, enjoy nature and meditate. I love playing cards and board games, challenging myself with Sudoku and code crackers, and constantly learning new things through study, reading and online courses. Most importantly, I do a check- up from the neck up regularly. Believe me, it is easy to slip off the track now and then, and hey, that's ok. It is how *long* you stay off- track that matters.

Learning new things expands that neuroplasticity in your brain. John Assaraf, in his book *'Innercise,'* which is aptly named, gives many suggestions and exercises. There are many ways to exercise your mind. Learning new things is a major accomplishment, learning a new language is a great one, it is one of my goals. Playing table tennis exercises the mind and body, using coordination of mind, eyes, arms and legs, as does learning new dance steps and, if it is with a partner, it can also bring in emotion.

I had to have a little giggle to myself here, because through personal experience, I have learnt that learning new dance steps with a partner can cause a bit of friction and frustration too, if one can't quite get it. But hang in there, as when it is fun and works, the emotions are good ones. Doing word or number puzzles, such as Sudoku and crosswords, playing card or board games, are deemed to be some of the best for exercising the brain.

Modern technology denies crucial exercise to certain parts of the brain in a couple of ways, causing it to waste slowly away. We are exposed to numerous sources of stimulation which disrupts the production of Acetylcholine, an organic chemical that functions in the brain and body as a neurotransmitter. It is released by nerve cells, to send signals to other cells.

Also, we no longer need to remember addresses, phone numbers, dates or basic navigation skills, because our phones and GPS's have replaced so much of our memories. Hence the need to learn new things; use it or lose it.

Even just changing doing things the same way all of the time will create new neural pathways. E.g. change the way you go to work, take another route. Try doing things, like cleaning your teeth with the opposite hand, get out of bed on the opposite side or sleeping on the other side.

Bottom line, what we consciously program into our mind, repeat and retain, becomes memories, not only in our mind, but throughout our body; it creates our reality. We are creating behavioural patterns, programs and habits, which in turn, just like a computer, if the wrong information is programmed in and not kept in check, it will get dis-ease and viruses.

Dis-ease within the body is simply thought in form. We create our dis-ease through our thinking. So, treating any dis-ease without treating the underlying thought is not curing the condition, it is only masking it. I am not by any means belittling doctors or **necessary** medicines, they have their place. Although the word 'Doctor' means 'Teacher', we do not see too much teaching happening. As Dr Ulric Williams said "The duty of the medical profession should be to teach people to be healthy." He said he never became a real doctor until he forgot 95% of what he learnt at Edinburgh medical school. However, I do believe if we learn how to look after our mind and body, we can avoid the medical system 99% of the time.

"There's no drug more powerful in the world than the mind"
The mind can create the symptom of every illness on the planet.
It can probably create every illness.
But if it created it, of course, it can also remove it.

Chapter 2
Conscious V's Subconscious Mind

The three levels of your mind 24
Your thoughts create your reality 27
You can change the channel 30
Your Inherent mental power 33
We all have choices 38

*"The MIND is connected to the brain; however,
It is undetected by any instrument.
The MIND is free to wonder, explore and create.
It is the elusive part of the brain that has the capability
to receive Telecommunication instantly.
It is also one of the most talked about, yet totally invisible,
parts of the human body.*

'AUTHOR Unknown'

The three levels of mind

You have only one mind, however it consists of three levels: *Conscious*, *Subconscious* and *Superconscious*. In this book we will mainly talk about the two that most people are aware of, the Conscious and Subconscious.

The **superconscious mind** is the higher level of consciousness; it encompasses a level of awareness that sees both material reality and also the energy and consciousness behind that reality. If you meditate and feel calm, then you are beginning to experience a level of super consciousness. I am not delving into this level in this book.

Your Conscious and Subconscious each have distinct attributes and powers.

As most people think in pictures, in the 1930s, Dr. Thurman Fleet of Texas USA developed a graphic image of our mind and body to provide a 'picture' to help his patients understand how the mind works relative to our thoughts.

I studied with Bob Proctor many years ago using Dr Fleets stickman.

I have created my stickman. As you can see, the image consists of a large circle at the top which represents the MIND and a small oval that represents the BODY. The circle that illustrates our MIND is in much greater proportion to the BODY because the MIND is so powerful and is responsible for our results in life. The BODY is merely a manifestation of what's going on in our mind, albeit a very

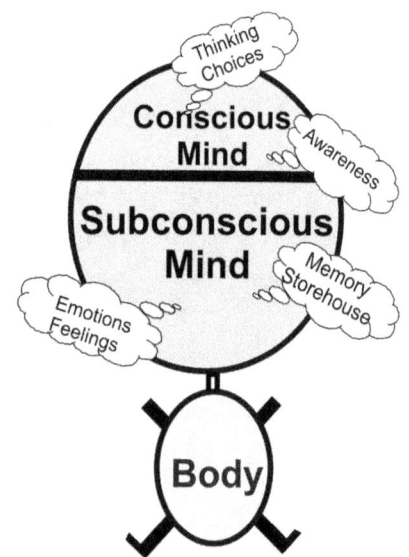

important part of us! It shows the MIND in two parts—the Conscious Mind and the Subconscious MIND, the latter being larger because it is our storehouse.

The **conscious mind,** or surface mind, is where your awareness lies; it's where you can choose your thoughts, whether positive or negative, building or destroying. Here you can accept, reject or neglect any thought you want.

For example, if someone compliments you, you might want to consciously accept that thought; once you accept it your mind will file it into your subconscious mind. If someone tells you you're worthless, you hopefully would reject that thought, hence it will not be filed away in your storehouse.

The Conscious mind is the part of the mind that we operate with during our daily activities and waking hours. It represents only a small portion of your consciousness and awareness. What you accept as true in the conscious mind passes onto our subconscious mind, this is the bodies doer. It overhears everything you think and say and then puts it into action.

It is interesting when you completely understand how we use our consciousness and how it affects your body.

Your body reacts internally to the vibrations of the energy of all of your senses, things you hear, see, smell, taste, touch. For example; if your doctor told you that you had a life-threatening condition, you might react with anger, fear or become depressed. Each of these energies will have a further affect within your body.

Anger affects your liver; fear affects your kidneys and depression affects your lungs and chest. Each of these organs has major jobs to do in your body and when added stress from these reactions/vibrational energies affects them, they will not function to their full capacity, hence impeding their ability to heal and counteract the dis-ease. I will expand on this in the next chapter.

The **subconscious mind,** or deeper mind, also called your Feeling or Emotional mind, lies below the level of conscious awareness. This is the storehouse for all of your memories, programs, emotions, self-image, paradigms and experiences; it is your *book of life*. It's where your belief system, habits and conditioned responses reside. It's a bit like a filing cabinet or Google. Unlike your conscious mind, it cannot reject...it must accept whatever thoughts or images you feed into it over and over again, creating new neural pathways or thickening old pathways.

Whether real or imagined, positive or negative, your subconscious mind doesn't know the difference; it just knows that you have consciously accepted it. It records everything you do; every activity we engage in, your thoughts about those activities, your likes and dislikes about what you encounter each day. Nothing is forgotten by the subconscious mind, and most of the time this part of your consciousness remains hidden from your everyday awareness. Your subconscious mind has a tremendous influence on how you think and act when in a conscious state; it remembers how you react emotionally to events you have experienced. It remembers the negative far easier than the positive, so you need to let go of negative and feed the positive.

One of your subconscious mind's most important functions is to keep you living in alignment with your ingrained habits and beliefs. In other words, keep you living inside your 'comfort zone'!

"It is the mark of an educated mind to be able to entertain a thought without accepting it."

'Aristotle'

Your thoughts create your reality

What happens is, when you even think about doing something out of the ordinary, your subconscious mind automatically goes into 'red alert mode' and produces emotions such as fear and discomfort, to encourage you to stay within the boundaries of your comfort zone. We will expand on this later.

Would you agree that it makes sense that if you can accept or reject any thought that comes into your Conscious Mind, it would be better to choose to focus on only the positive of even the worst situation? Of course, it does!

Because your **thoughts** cause your **feelings**, your **feelings** move your body into **action** and your **actions** produce…yes that's right, your **RESULTS** in life!

Every thought is a cause and every condition is an effect.

Did you know that it takes more energy to be sad, down and out, than to be happy? It takes more effort and uses more muscles to frown than to smile. So, keep smiling and produce those happy hormones and smile lines, not frown lines; energise yourself.

So, what influences our Conscious Mind?

You have five physical senses that have tremendous influence over your thoughts. You see, hear, smell, taste and touch. But when you rely solely on your physical senses to influence your thinking, your emotions can be like a cork bobbing on water.

For example, if you **see** something funny on the television, see a baby laugh, or a puppy playing, listen to music you love, you **feel** happy. Right? Five minutes later, you could be talking to someone who insults you and immediately you change from happy to angry or hurt.

You **hear** bad news; you have someone close to you pass away and you feel sad. You **touch** a hot element or cut yourself you **feel** sore, you enjoy a kiss, a hug - the **touch** of a loved one and **feel** loved. You **smell** something putrid you turn away, **smell** a rose you enjoy. You **Taste** a sour lemon and screw up your face or a juicy sweet orange and say yummy. We all constantly change emotions with each different circumstance that we encounter through our physical senses. We experience fun, fear, happy, sad, exhilarated, feel tired, we laugh, we cry.

You are the captain of your ship, you need to be the navigator, giving the right orders (thoughts and images) to your subconscious mind which controls and governs all of your experiences.

Whatever you want, you need to convey to your subconscious mind with love and feelings and it will obey. Never use the words "I can't afford or" or "I can't do this" as your subconscious mind takes you at your word and sees to it that you will not or cannot do or have what you want. Affirm to yourself, "I *can* do and have all of the things I want through the power of my subconscious mind. Say it often and with feeling and passion and see what changes in your life.

When I wake up every morning, I say to myself, "I am so happy and grateful that I have so much love happiness in my life. I am so healthy and fit and everything comes to me as I need it. I am and it does." You are creating your life, whether you realise it or not.

Because others cannot vibrate in your experience, they cannot affect the outcome of your experience.
They can hold their opinions, but unless their opinion affects your opinion, their opinion matters not at all.
A million people could be pushing against you and it Would

not affect you unless you push back.
That millions of people pushing against you, are affecting their millions of vibrations.
They are affecting what is happening in their experience.
They are affecting their point of attraction, but it does not affect you unless you push back.

'Abraham'

You can change the channel

Since the day you were born, your conscious mind has been constantly bombarded with messages via your physical senses.

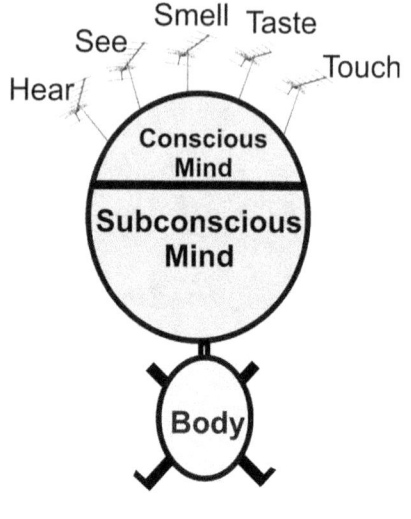

These senses are like little antennae, hard-wired right into your mind! With your conscious mind, your physical senses bring in information, whether positive or negative. It is not only how we think about these messages or sensations that are coming into your conscious mind, it is also how we react to them that creates our results. And everyone interprets things differently.

Many of us hold onto the past and let it affect our lives for many years. We will discuss how that affects us later.

As previously mentioned, if you don't like what you are seeing or hearing, you can change the channel; you don't have to listen to or take on board what others say or do. You have to do what you think is right for you, what is aligned to your values; always tap into, go with and follow your intuition.

As I have previously said and will repeat, you need to do a check-up from the neck up regularly, think how you are thinking, and watch what you are putting into your mind, because it creates your reality. Look after your mind; it is more powerful than you can ever imagine; more powerful than any computer. It can store more information than a computer, so you need to do a software upgrade on it now and then. Exercise, feed and look after your mind.

You could relate your subconscious mind to a filing cabinet or Google. Everything you have read, thought, seen, experienced, is filed away in your subconscious mind, just waiting to be referred to. One of the main problems is that our conscious mind keeps getting in the way, but the answers are all there. Have you ever tried to think of a name, or where you left something and the more you try to recall it, the more frustrated you get? That is because it is filed away in your subconscious mind and you are thinking with your conscious mind which is blocking the way to the filing cabinet. If that happens, just say 'it will come to me in a minute,' stop thinking about it, think of something else and it will come to you in no time.

We just need to get out of our own way every now and then, stop thinking too hard with our conscious mind and allow our subconscious mind to deliver.

Exams are also a good example of us getting in our own way, blocking the answers. The above technique can be used well in exams. I always believed that I was useless at school exams. I tried to think too hard and never felt confident, I was in my own way. When I went nursing, doing something I loved and was interested in, I did well, I had retained my learning well and could recall them. I always remember our tutor the day before our exams, saying "there is no use studying tonight, go to the movies and relax. If you don't know it now you never will". The answers will come to you when you need them, you just need to ask, think of something else and wait for the answer. Remember, everything you have learnt, read or seen is filed away in that filing cabinet in your subconscious mind.

"The knowledge of the interaction of your conscious and subconscious minds will enable you to transform your whole life."

'Dr Joseph Murphy'

Your inherent mental power

You just learnt that your Conscious Mind is constantly bombarded with messages via your physical senses. However, there is another effective way for you to influence your own thinking, rather than relying on your physical senses. It is to look within, to the higher side of your nature, your mental power!

You have six mind power abilities which you can tap into; Bob Proctor called them *mental muscles*. When you develop, understand and use these abilities, your life will change forever!

Your Mind Power abilities are Perception, Will, Imagination, Memory, Intuition, and Reason. So, let's look at each of these and how we use them.

Perception: When we change our perception, the way we look at things, things change. Your perception is only your own belief or opinion, based on how you see or view things. Each person's perception can vary considerably to others. Your reality is just how you perceive things, how you have viewed whatever through your perception.

How do you perceive the size of anything? Big v's small- You have to measure it against something else. A big house, a small house, a big child a small child.

Nothing is big or small, old or young, fat or thin, good or bad unless it is judged or measured against something or someone else. Everything just is.

What do you see in the pictures above?

Everyone sees different images, what they see is their perception.

The power of placebo is an interesting concept that is so real that people perceive it to be true.

I remember when I was nursing in my teens, sugar pills were sometimes given to someone who perceived they were in severe pain. When given a sugar pill and taken with the belief that it was a real pain killer, it took away the pain. They told their brain that they had taken pain relief, so the brain told the body and it worked, the pain was gone. An amazing perception, don't you think?

One person's pain could be perceived as severe, another could be experiencing the same level but perceive it differently, depending on their tolerance of pain.

A piece of paper may have nothing on one side, information on the other – two people could look at it from different sides, each gets a different perception. There are two sides to a coin, people may see different things in the same picture, read a word or sentence and get a different meaning. It happens all of the time; life is so interesting.

Is it really cold in winter and hot in summer? It depends on what country you live in or are visiting, what you are accustomed to or how thick or thin your blood is as to how you feel the cold or heat. Some say blue is a cold colour; others will say it is a warm healing colour. And, so it goes on, everything you see, judge, experience is just how you perceive it. So, look on the bright side, look for the positive in everything, and don't judge others for their perception as it is only their perception and maybe not yours. Everything just is.

Will: Using your 'will', meaning the inner power to really want it to have, do or be, gives you the ability to stay focused, to concentrate. To concentrate on one thing, on a desire, purpose or outcome, it is your determination. I believe I have the ability to heal myself and I have the will to do so. Do you? Because you can if you have the will.

Will is to the mind like a magnifying glass is to the sun – The sun will burn faster focused through a magnifying glass than the sun on a body when lying in it because of focus.

Imagination: Everything starts in your imagination. Edison said ***"Imagination is more powerful and important than knowledge."*** That is how he illuminated the world and how man landed on the moon. When we develop reason, we lose our imagination.

Everything started with imagination in the mind, a thought – the chair you are sitting on was once an image in someone's imagination as previously mentioned, it was a thought.

You can imagine your life happy, healthy and fun or hard and sad. Your choice.

Your imagination can create heaven or hell in your life. Your imagination, if used wrongly, can stop so many good things. It creates fear and causes so many phobias of what might happen. On the other hand, it can be amazing if you turn it around and imagine fantastic outcomes.

Memory: Bob Proctor says "Everyone has a perfect memory – However, we say and feel that we haven't, so we haven't!!!"

With the power of our memory, we can choose to remember all of the good or the bad. Unfortunately, most choose to remember and relive bad experiences and they leave impressions in the mind easier than good experiences and take more effort to erase and let go. Use it or lose it; use your memory to serve you.

Keep telling yourself that your memory is getting better and better all of the time.

Can you remember what is on the back of a 50cent coin or a $20 note? Most people can't, we need to be aware, notice the little things, we see things every day but don't observe.

Intuition: is your 6th sense, this is where your hunches come from, your gut feelings.

We often say – we got a good or bad vibe from someone – that's our intuition, we are picking up the energy from that person. We are constantly picking up and giving out good or bad energy. Intuition is when we become aware of vibrations and signs.

If prayer is us talking to God (the Universe) then intuition is God (the Universe) talking to us.

The problem with intuition is that many of us use it wrongly. We often don't take notice of our thoughts and feelings that are trying to tell us something. When an idea comes into our mind, we continually ask the wrong questions – we ask ourselves, is it good or bad, is it the right or wrong thing to do? Should I, or shouldn't I? A good question to ask is – If I act on this, will it help me move towards the outcome I want? Or will it give me the results I require?

If it feels right, just do it. Act on it, don't question it. It is your intuition, your gut feeling.

We keep judging and pushing intuition away. If we ask others their opinion, the answer will only be their perception. Go with your intuition. Kinesiology, or muscle testing, is a good way to test things we are unsure of; it is tapping into our body's intuitive senses.

Reason: This is the part of us that separates us from an animal; this is our ability to choose. We can gather independent facts and come to our own conclusion, or we can start with a conclusion and go out and collect the facts. This is our free will.

This mental ability helps us to change the way we think.

Learn them, use them, it will create a great awareness within.

"Everything can be taken from a man but one thing: the last of the human freedoms to choose one's attitude in any given set of circumstances, to choose one's own way."

'Viktor Frankl'

We all have choices

You must remember that you have two spheres of activity in your mind, your conscious and subconscious. Your conscious mind is your reasoning mind where you can make choices. For example: you choose your house, your car, the food you eat, your partner, what book to read or TV program you want to watch. You make all of your decisions with your conscious mind.

On the other hand, without any conscious choice on your part, your heart keeps pumping, you breathe, digest food, your blood circulates automatically. These processes are carried out by your subconscious mind, independent from your conscious control. But remember that your subconscious mind also accepts whatever you impress on it, what you choose to believe. It is a bit like soil that accepts any kind of seed, good or bad; your subconscious mind accepts what you believe, what you consciously plant in it. It doesn't try to prove whether something is right or wrong, or make comparisons. Neither does it reason or think things out for itself, it simply responds according to your thoughts and suggestions from your conscious mind.

For example, if you consciously assume something is true, even if it is false, your subconscious mind will accept it as true and file that belief away for future reference. Or, if someone puts the suggestion in your mind that if you go out on a boat you will get seasick and you choose to believe it, then you will for sure. However, you can reject that thought and you will be fine.

A suggestion in itself has no power unless you accept it mentally. Remember that your subconscious mind cannot take a joke; it takes you at your word.

If you choose to look at everything as **'Just is'** and not judge as good or bad, right or wrong, life is much easier.

Have you heard the following saying? *'When you change the way you look at things, things change.'* Changing the way you look at things is a great way to change fear, worry or repetitive thinking of an event, something that has happened to you in the past, that you continually remind yourself of because when it happened you perceived it as not acceptable, dangerous, disturbing, negative, or whatever.

We tend to hold onto old hurts, negative events and fears that we have created in our subconscious mind. We keep reliving, replaying them over and over in our mind and the more we replay an image, it embeds itself deeper in our sub conscious mind. It often changes slightly each time you replay it, just like a Chinese whisper. Sometimes it grows bigger and appears worse in your mind. This does not serve you; it is holding you prisoner and often causes Dis-ease.

An exercise you can try is to look at an unpleasant event as a movie; change the scenes (the meaning of it) and let it go. "Let go" are two very important little words. If you don't change the meaning of the scene and let go of it, you may keep holding onto it and the movie will keep playing in your mind. It will continue to cause you grief and create dis-ease in your mind and body. Life is too short to be living in the past with fear, anger and resentment.

When you understand and grasp the power within you and you use it, it is amazing. Don't allow others to take you off track. With proper use of your mental power, blended with thought and feeling, you can gain control of your emotional mind, then you begin to move your body into greater feelings and positive vibrations.

Here is an example- You could be made redundant; you could start to feel angry, sad, get emotional, feel fear, think bad things. Such as: "I've lost my job, there will be no money coming in. How will I survive? How can they do this to me? Poor me, poor me!" Or you could see it as a positive happening – You could start doing what you really enjoy doing; Start thinking and believing there is something better out there for you; say to yourself "I deserve more money and a better job and will find something I love doing with better pay. Or I will be able to have the holiday I have been waiting for." Everything happens for a reason.

As I mentioned earlier, your thoughts cause your feelings, your feelings are expressed in actions, and your actions produce your results. So, if you want to control what is going on on the outside, you also have to control what is going on on the inside.

Remember, you have choices; you have the power within to make changes.

When we do exercises and strengthen our body muscles, our biceps, triceps, shoulders, breathing exercises for our lungs, we feel great, right? The more exercise you do, the better and fitter you feel, so long as you don't start by over doing it. If you try too hard to begin with you may put yourself off and give up.

If you laze around all day being a couch potato, you feel sluggish right? Well you also need to do mental exercises, to strengthen your brain muscles, your neuro muscles, to keep them active and alert. As the saying goes- use it or lose it. When you exercise your mind, your Neuro muscles, you feel more alert and healthier. By exercising your mind, you will also change habits, self-talk and destructive thinking.

The trouble with many people is that they **believe** what is going on in their mind all day long, what they are telling themselves, and the mind chatter that is continuously happening. Guess what? Most of what is going on in your mind is not necessarily your truth. That mind chatter is the same every day and is often something that has been planted in your mind by someone else; your parents, teachers, siblings, partner, peers, the newspapers, radio & TV, social media. You have chosen to believe it. Or you are worrying about something that you either have no control over, or something you need to take action on, but are procrastinating with for some reason.

If you have a belief and you are unsure of it, question it. Ask yourself, do I really believe it? Then ask 'Why do I believe it'? A belief is not necessarily a truth, it is often just something you have heard and chosen to believe. So, question it.

Remember, your subconscious mind has no ability to reject thoughts... it must accept whatever images are fed into it via your conscious mind or what you have accepted, believed and allowed in from outside influences. The more you think of something, the more ingrained it is into your subconscious mind. Hence, you need to monitor your thoughts; Yes, do a check-up from the neck up regularly and check on those repetitive thoughts.

Every result you have in your life starts with your thoughts. Remember, everything you do creates a neural pathway in your subconscious mind and every time you repeat an action or words, you make that neural pathway thicker, forming a habit, an impression or belief.

Here is an analogy that depicts the way your mind operates.

A farmer has good fertile land; the land gives the farmer a choice, He can plant and let grow whatever he chooses. The land doesn't care; it is up for the farmer to make the decision. Remember, we are comparing the mind with the land, because the mind, just like the land, doesn't care what you plant in it. It will return what you plant. That's right, it doesn't care what you plant. The farmer can take two seeds, one a corn seed and the other a weed, nightshade, a deadly poison. He can poke two little holes in the soil and plant both seeds, cover up the holes, give them water and take care of the land.

So, what happens? Yes, they both grow. As you sow, so shall you reap, remember the land doesn't care, it will return weeds just as well as it will good healthy food; it makes no difference to the land.

The human mind is far more fertile, far more incredible than the land, but it works the same way, it doesn't care whether you plant seeds of success or failure, good or bad, but it makes all the difference to you; to the harvest you will reap in your life. The seeds you plant in your mind will determine your life, what you plant will grow, good, bad, happy, sad, success or failure.

Imagine your mind as a garden. Do you want it looking great or full of weeds? You have a choice. If you plant good seeds (thoughts), continue to nurture them (repeat, repeat the good thoughts) and pull out the weeds (eradicate the ANT'S).Imagine the great harvest you will have, a fantastic, happy, healthy mind, full of good thoughts, hence a happy healthy body if you are also feeding it good food and exercising it.

Another analogy is the acorn. Every acorn has the potential to turn into an oak tree, but only a few actually do. Just like your brain, an acorn needs nourishment; fertile soil (positive thinking), water, nutrient (Good food and relationships) and the sun to become a mighty oak tree. Without all of these nurturing components working in harmony, the acorn will not survive and grow into that mighty oak.

You have the ability to choose every moment of the day. So, choose to be positive, with happiness, peace and harmony and see how your life changes.

"What lies behind us and what lies before us are tiny matters Compared to what lies within us."

'Oliver Wendell Holmes'

Chapter 3
You Become What You Think About

Your mind does what it thinks you want 45
Your happiness chemicals 49
Thoughts affect your health.. 54
Medical histories are like peering into a crystal ball 58

*"Every human has four endowments; self-awareness,
conscience, independent will and creative imagination.
These give us the ultimate human freedom.
The power to choose, to respond, to change."*

'Stephen Covey'

Your mind does what it thinks you want

You BECOME what you THINK ABOUT most of the time; life is a mirror and will reflect back to you what you put out there. Positive attracts positive just as quickly as negative attracts negative.

'Abracadabra' is considered to be the most universally adopted phrase that is pronounced in other languages without translation –'I will create as I speak'.

I will repeat the following words again and again as it is so important and we learn by repetition. One of the most important things you need to get your head around is that *"the words you constantly use, whether talking to yourself or to others, and the pictures you create in your mind, create your life, your reality"*. This is so profound when you really get it, when you think about what is happening in your mind day and night and you think about what is happening in your life, it usually matches up.

Here is a real-life example: My mother was living on her own, I would telephone her regularly and pop into see her now and then. (I lived about an hour away). Every time I spoke to her and ask how she was, she would say, 'I am fine, except this dammed thing on my leg won't go away'. Sure enough, it wouldn't, she had an ulcer on her leg, for eight months, every second day she went to the doctor's clinic to have it dressed and it never improved.

There are two lessons here: firstly, when you give something lots of attention and call it 'mine' you own it, and secondly, what you continually say to yourself and others is what you get. Mum came to live with me and the first thing I said to her when she moved in with me was 'ok we are going to fix this ulcer'. As a healer, I gave it good energy and sunlight. I told mum not to talk about it to other people and if they asked how it was, just to say it is getting better and better every day. From that day on, she repeated daily, 'it is getting better and better every day.' The ulcer started shrinking in no time and healed completely in a few weeks.

Just as your consciousness can create dis-ease within your body, it can also heal if you take control of it. We can transform energy if we know how. Firstly, just know and believe that your thoughts are energy, a creative force and as I repeat many times in this book, you create your life by the words you use and the pictures you create in your mind.

So, if you have dis-ease in your mind or body, you need to go within and ask for help to heal; ask your higher self, your God, the universe or whatever deity you believe in. Believe that you can heal, will heal, and open all channels (simply say they are open) to allow healing to happen. Meditate, go within and ask the question what do I need to change in my life, in my thinking to turn my dis-ease around? Or what is my thinking that has caused my Dis-ease? Your higher self, your subconscious mind, will know. If you get out of your own way, out of your conscious mind and into your subconscious mind the answer will come, it will be the first thing that enters your mind. Then take action to change your life.

It is important to be flexible in your life, relax and take it easy knowing your body can and will heal. We often get mad at what someone else does or says. We worry and judge others because they are not like us. All of these actions not only hurt others, but they also hurt us, they cause Dis-ease. You can change your attitude easily if you choose to. We all have choices. You will find that life will be a much smoother road, if and when you do.

If you find yourself reacting negatively in a situation, take long slow breaths, relax, breath through your heart space and send love, kindness and forgiveness to everyone and everything. Do this and your life will change, not only in that moment, but forever. Believe me, it is a wonderful feeling.

Many of your thoughts are repetitious, day after day, especially if you are worried about something. Sometimes, it could be continuous year after year, if you are holding onto something from the past. It is important to realise that your mind doesn't know the difference between true or false, positive or negative, real or imagined, it just takes on board what you keep telling yourself, like the movies you play in your mind. Because you are continuously giving that movie so much attention, it becomes real to your subconscious mind and what it thinks you want. When you concentrate on a dis- ease, it will persist, your subconscious will obey. It is called dis-ease consciousness.

So, what are you telling yourself? What's going on in your mind? I challenge you to commit to healthy thinking, to be conscious of what is going on in your mind and how often the same things keep coming to mind.

Let's look further at how your thoughts affect your health. Your thoughts control your blood flow, that's why when you get embarrassed, you blush. Your thoughts can cause stress, anxiety, tension, increase your blood pressure and heart rate or they can promote health, fun, love and happiness. They can affect your self-esteem incredibly.

Your mind does what it thinks you want, what you tell it to do. Its job is to keep you alive by avoiding pain. The only possible way it can know what causes you pain is what you tell it. And once you tell it things, it locks onto them.

So here's an example - Imagine you're driving to work in heavy traffic which is the norm anywhere in the world now. Your saying to yourself, "OMG, this traffic is hell, it really is a nightmare," "and I have to complete that assignment that is driving me up the wall. I am so stressed all the time, it's driving me insane." This thinking starts your mind going, "hmmm, what's happening here?"...., I am continually hearing, "Hell, nightmare, stress" and reacts with - "I'm the mind, it's my job to keep you safe and alive, and you keep talking about something that's always stressing you and driving you insane. So, it's your job, you hate it, you don't want to go there! Leave that with me. My job is to keep you away from pain, so I'll have to make you sick so you can't go back to that job." Hence you get a migraine, back ache, dysentery, the flue....... Need I say more?

"Never change your originality for the sake of others
Because no one can play your role better than you.
Be yourself. You are the best"
"Besides you can't be anybody else, everybody else is taken"

Your happiness chemicals

The difference between success and failure, health or dis-ease, is not how you look. It's not how you dress. It's not even how you are educated. So, what is it? It's HOW YOU THINK!

Your mind is so powerful, it can create almost any dis-ease on the planet, which stands to reason if it can create it, it can also cure almost any dis-ease on the planet. Just like the watchmaker that made your watch knows how to fix it.

We have many psychological barriers that compromise our health; emotions and impulses arising from within, from outside influences and memories stored in our subconscious mind. Also, emotions such as fear, resentment, self-pity, jealousy, worry, pride, materialism, lust, together with any negative thoughts, beliefs acting out from your subconscious mind and they will all play havoc with your health if not checked. Remember that regular check up from the neck up.

The great thing is that you have choices; you can choose to have a happy healthy life and work towards it, or not! You have four neurotransmitters or so-called happiness chemicals in your body that are responsible for your happiness and look forward to working for you if you choose to use them. They are Dopamine, Serotonin, Oxytocin, and Endorphins. Many situations can trigger these neurotransmitters, so instead of being in the passenger seat, there are ways you can be in the front seat, be the driver and intentionally get them flowing. You can set your sails and steer your ship or, if you prefer, be the Architect of your life. We all have choices.

We will talk about the basics of healthy living in part 2.

Meanwhile, let us look at our 'happy chemicals'.

Being in a positive state of mind has a significant impact on your motivation, productivity and wellbeing. Here are some simple ways to get your happy chemicals flowing:

Dopamine is your motivator to take action toward your goals; it gives you a surge of reinforcing pleasure when you achieve them. Studies have shown that procrastination, self-doubt, and lack of enthusiasm are linked to low levels of dopamine. If you set goals, then break them down into little pieces. You can celebrate your achievements more often rather than only allowing your brain to celebrate when you've hit the big finish line. When you pat yourself on the back with each mini goal you achieve, you create a good feeling within.

Continue to create new goals before achieving your current one to ensure a consistent pattern for experiencing dopamine and stay motivated. You won't procrastinate as much.

Serotonin flows when you feel significant or important. Loneliness and depression are present when serotonin is absent. If you go back in time, we all belonged to tribes; it is in our DNA to want to belong. That is why people fall into gangs and criminal activity, the culture and 'community' facilitate serotonin release, giving a feeling of belonging. Unhealthy attention-seeking behaviours are also a cry for what serotonin provides. Neuroscientist, Barry Jacobs says that most antidepressants focus on the production of serotonin.

Reflecting on your past achievements allows your brain to re-live the experience. As previously mentioned, your brain has trouble telling the difference between what is real or imagined, so it produces serotonin in both cases, hence imagining great things happening will raise your serotonin level. Gratitude practices are popular for this reason; they are reminders, mental pictures of all the good things you've experienced. If you need a serotonin boost during a stressful day, take a few moments to reflect on your past achievements and victories. If you don't feel that you have achieved anything of significance then imagine doing something you have always wanted to do or being someone you admire. Close your eyes and imagine you are in your favourite place in nature. It works.

Another way to boost your serotonin levels is to expose yourself to the sun for twenty minutes daily; your skin absorbs UV rays which promotes Vitamin-D and serotonin production. Mind that you don't over expose yourself to the sun as too much ultraviolet light isn't good.

Foods that produce and boost serotonin are complex carbohydrates, such as sweet potatoes, apples, blueberries, carrots, and chick peas. Brain **serotonin** levels can also be raised by **eating foods** rich in L-tryptophan, such as chicken, turkey, salmon, beef, pineapple, tofu, cheese, green peas, nuts and seeds and eggs. According to recent research, the protein in eggs can significantly boost your blood plasma levels of tryptophan. Tryptophan is an essential amino acid that serves several important purposes, like nitrogen balance in adults and growth in infants. It also creates niacin, which is essential in creating serotonin.

Your 3rd Happy Chemical, *Oxytocin*, is often referred to as "the cuddle hormone," a simple way to keep oxytocin flowing is to hug someone. I love hugs. I always greet people with a hug, unless I get the feeling that they are not into hugs, which some people aren't. You can even hug yourself, a soft cuddly bear or a pet. The release of oxytocin creates intimacy, trust, and strengthens relationships. It's released by men and women during an orgasm, and by mothers during childbirth and breastfeeding. Oxytocin is the glue that binds together healthy relationships.

Dr. Paul Zak, a pioneer in the field of Neuro economics, says "the hormone oxytocin promotes trust, and proving that love is good for everyone including business." He explains that inter-personal touch not only raises oxytocin, but reduces cardiovascular stress and improves the immune system. Rather than just a hand-shake, go in for the hug. He recommends eight hugs each day.

Giving someone a gift, will also cause their oxytocin levels to rise. You can strengthen work and personal relationships through a simple birthday or anniversary gift.

Endorphins are the 4th happy chemical; they are released in response to pain and stress, and helps to alleviate anxiety. The surging 'second wind' and euphoric 'runners high' when runners run a marathon are a result of endorphins. Similar to morphine, it acts as an analgesic and sedative, diminishing your perception of pain.

Along with exercise, laughter is one of the easiest ways to induce endorphin release. Even just a smile or the anticipation and expectation of laugher e.g. attending a comedy show or watching a funny movie increases levels of endorphins. Taking your sense of humour to work, forwarding that funny email, and finding several things to laugh at during the day is a great way to keep your endorphins flowing. Or just laugh for no reason at all. It works. Try it, smile, then start laughing. You end up laughing at yourself; it's fun.

I often get people to smile when they are feeling down as it changes your endorphins. Many say I can't, I have nothing to smile about, so I get them to hold a pen between their teeth, which tricks their body into thinking they are smiling and produces endorphins. They usually end up smiling because they think they look stupid, so it works.

The smell of vanilla and lavender has been linked with the production of endorphins. Studies have shown that dark chocolate and spicy foods will also cause your brain to release endorphins. Keep some scented oils and dark chocolate (but not too much ☺) on hand for a quick endorphin boost.

*"The mind is the source of all suffering,
And it is also the source of all happiness."*

Pema Chodron

Thoughts affect your health

Your body has its defences to combat dis-ease within. It will respond amazingly to most abnormalities that poke their head up and, given the right conditions and thinking, will do its best to survive. If you put diesel in a petrol motor, or don't give it oil, your car will not perform. Same goes for your body. Give it a healthy way of living and it will look after you.

You have just read about your happy chemicals and how they affect your health. Let's expand on that a little: When all of your happy hormones are working well, you are more positive. Positive thinking produces chemicals in the brain and cells of the central nervous system. This then produces Natural Killer (NK) cells, which can destroy certain types of illness, tumours and fight bacteria and viruses, keeping you healthy and resilient. It is documented that people have cured themselves of cancer just by laughing, or continuously watching funny movies. Of course, along with feeding their mind good thoughts, you also need to feed your body the right foods and exercise, which we will go into a little later.

NK cells were identified in 1975 as lymphocytes of the innate immune system that can kill tumour cells. Since then, NK cells have been shown to kill an array of 'stressed' cells and secrete cytokines that participate in shaping adaptive immune responses. A key feature of NK cells resides in their capacity to distinguish stressed cells (such as tumour cells, infected and damaged cells) from normal cells. I will not get into in-depth technical details as that is far from my expertise. You can check out Mr Google for more information.

Always remember the power of your mind. It is so powerful and with the will to do so, you can control it. It takes discipline, but you can do it. Remember, 'Your mind does what it thinks you want, what you tell it to do. Its job is to keep you alive by avoiding pain. Your thoughts do affect your health. Remember, the words you say and the pictures you create in your mind, create your reality'.

Anything, whether it is food, drugs, thoughts, people, events or words that are not good for you can weaken you and if experienced for a prolonged period, will make you ill, creating dis-ease in your body one way or another. Don Tolman, America's Whole Foods Guru says: 'If you are in an unhealthy relationship, I will give you 5 minutes to get out of it.' Unhealthy relationships are a major cause of dis-ease.

Negative thoughts, food and people all diminish your energy.

Positive people, food and thoughts will energise you. We talk more about this in part 2.

Remember Dr. Amen's Ant's in chapter one- keep those thoughts positive.

The late Louise Hay and Inna Segal are two amazing healers and authors that have influenced my life. Both have produced books on the language of your body and how your thoughts create illness and dis-ease within.

Louise Hay, in her book *'Heal Your Body,'* gives an ailment, possible thoughts that have created it and affirmations to say to change your thinking. Her book *'Heal Your Body A-Z'* is based on her bestseller *Heal Your Body*. Louise shows you that, if you are willing to do the mental work, almost anything can be healed. Just look up your specific health challenge and you will find the probable cause for the issue, as well as the information you need to overcome it by creating a new thought pattern. The list of mental equivalents in this book has been compiled from Louise's many years of study, her work with clients, and her lectures and workshops. You will find that *Heal Your Body A-Z* is invaluable as a quick-reference guide to the probable mental patterns behind the dis-ease in your body.

Inna Segal's book *'The Secret Language of Your Body,'* is also a comprehensive guide to healing. Inna unveils the secrets to understanding the messages of the body and reveals the underlying energetic causes of over 200 symptoms and medical conditions. This powerful handbook explores nearly every conceivable part of the human body, delving deeply into the possible reasons for problems in any given area of the body and offering a unique, step-by-step method to assist in returning the body to its natural state of health.

These are both amazing books that I have used for many years and given many away to family and friends. Of course there are the sceptics and there always will be. We are all on our own journey. However, I have proven many of their suggestions personally, as well as with clients.

The following is one of life's great lessons:

One evening, an old Cherokee told his son about the battle that goes on inside people.

He said, "My son, the battle is about two wolves that live inside of us all.

One is Evil – it is anger, envy, jealously, sorrow, regret, greed, arrogance, self-pity, guilt, resentment, inferiority, lies, false pride, superiority and ego.

The other is Good— it is joy, peace, love, hope, serenity, humility, kindness, benevolence, empathy, generosity, truth, compassion and faith."

The grandson thought about it for a minute, he then asked "which wolf wins?"

The old Cherokee replied, "The one you feed."

> "As a single footstep will not make a path on the earth,
> so a single thought will not make a pathway in the mind.
> To make a deep physical path, we walk again and again.
> To make a deep mental path, we must think over and over the
> kind of thoughts we wish to dominate our lives."
>
> 'Henry David Thoreau'

Medical histories are like peering into a crystal ball

Many people think they are destined for a dis-ease because "it's in the family!"

Looking at your relatives' medical histories is like peering into a crystal ball. You get a glimpse at your future, but not the whole picture. You can't change the genes you inherited, but you can avoid habits that contributed to your family's health problems. Look at a family dis-ease as a warning sign, a sign of what to do or what not to do. If you think you will contract a particular dis-ease, you more than likely will. If you always find a way of why you can't get better, you won't. Your mind does what it thinks you want, what you continually think and worry about.

As I said in Chapter 1, my life would be doomed if I believed that certain dis-eases were genetic with what has happened in my family.

Here is another real-life story about concentrating on what you don't want.

My mother had an elderly friend in her life for about 12 years. We will call him Harry for this story. Harry was in his early 80's and mum in her mid-70s when they meet. Mum was always looking after other people. She taught blind and visually impaired people to play bowls; she had lady friends in rest homes that she ran around after and tried to keep motivated; she did volunteer work constantly. She took Harry, who was visually impaired, under her wing and they became very close. Harry's wife (we will call her Mary) was in a rest home with Alzheimer's. She didn't recognize anyone anymore, but they visited her regularly. After a few years, mum and Harry's friendship got closer and they travelled and spent a lot of time together. Harry would sing to mum and always put on a great front when people were around, but when we got to know him better, we realised he had quite a nasty streak and was very rude to mum at times.

Mum put up with it because he was company and she also felt sorry for him with his impaired vision. Harry started telling mum that she was getting like his wife and she should go check out people who know about Alzheimer's. Mum would say to me when I visited 'I am so scared of becoming like Mary, don't ever let me live like that.' I would say to her "Don't listen to him mum, you are fine." But mum spent more time with Harry than me and continuously worried and focused on not getting Alzheimer's. (remember, what you focus on you are likely to get, your mind doesn't hear the NOT) By the way, Harry's family wouldn't speak to him unless they had to. They blamed him for their mothers Alzheimer's. I didn't believe them at first, but now do. I sincerely believe that he planted the seeds in her mind and watered them.

With repetition, we certainly do confirm things in our mind. So with Harry frequently repeating it and Mum worrying about it, it was inevitable. (The words we say to ourselves and the pictures we create in our mind, create our reality)

Then, the only two friends mum had left and had been caring for, passed away within 6 months of each other. All of a sudden, mum got paranoid about losing it and she was becoming lost and lonely. She was in a space she didn't want to be and went downhill very fast, constantly panicking. As I was in another town and busy with my life, I wasn't there for her as much as she needed and I didn't see it coming. She had always been so active and independent that I was used to her doing her own thing and not having to worry about her too much.

Ouch! A hard lesson for me and you: Look after your elderly parents and take notice of any changes. Mum came to live with me, but by this time, the Alzheimer's had taken hold.

Louise Hay and Inna Segal describe Alzheimer's and Dementia as Loss of power, an inability to deal with life, having too many suppressed emotions, wanting to run away, feeling lost and confused, anxiety living life the way it is. (Their descriptions can be all or any of what is mentioned)

Many elderly people are lonely, especially after losing a close friend or lifelong partner. They grieve, sometimes for the rest of their life. They become lost and afraid and withdraw themselves. If only they realised that there is still life to be lived. If only they could change their mind set and take control of their mind instead of allowing it to control them. I am sure their loved one would want them to remember the good, smile when they think of them and move on.

I know I grieved for my father and sister for many years and didn't even want to go to funerals. I didn't allow it to control my life, but tears came to my eyes frequently and they flowed at funerals. I wrote a Biography of my sister which helped immensely and then I became a funeral celebrant and helped people through their grief. Tears are still hard to hold back at times (that's called being human), but I am now in control and know that my loved ones are with me in spirit.

Your mindset and actions toward diet, lifestyle and environment cause 70% of your dis-ease. Your choices matter- where you live, your work, the people you spend most of your time with, what you put in your mouth, they all matter. Your genetics may load the gun but your lifestyle pulls the trigger. Dis-ease is a divine tap on your shoulder saying your lifestyle, the way you are living, could be making you ill, maybe even slowly killing you. I am not telling you this to shame you, just to let you know, or remind you, that it is time to take full responsibility for your life. There is always time to make changes, you are never too old.

> "The mind has exactly the same power as the hands;
> Not merely to grasp the world, but to change it."
>
> 'Colin Wilson'

Chapter 4
Your Mind Loves Familiarity and Habits

Repetition forms familiarity and habits 63

What is a habit? 65

Change your habits, change your life 70

Fear 75

> "The brick walls are not there to keep us out;
> The brick walls are there to give us a chance to show
> how badly we want something."
>
> 'Randy Pausch'

Repetition forms familiarity and habits

Do you remember the old saying – 'If you keep doing the same thing, you will keep getting the same results'? So if you are not happy and healthy, then you have work to do.

Think about it; it stands to reason, that if you can change your thoughts and actions, you are going to have a new experience. But one thing you need to know, one thing that holds you stuck in a place you don't want to be, is that your mind loves what is familiar and it doesn't like unfamiliar.

If left to its own devices, your mind always wants to go back to what it knows; it wants to avoid what is unfamiliar. If you want to make successful changes in your life, you have got to make what is familiar unfamiliar and what's unfamiliar, familiar. So, don't beat yourself up, just choose to take control of your mind.

One of your subconscious mind's most important functions is to keep you living in alignment with your embedded habits and beliefs. In other words, keep living inside your 'comfort zone'!

So, what happens is, when you even THINK about doing something out of the ordinary, your subconscious mind automatically goes into 'red alert mode' and produces emotions such as fear and discomfort, to encourage you to stay within the boundaries of your comfort zone.

Do you understand what I'm saying? I hope so. Think of a habit you currently have that you would like to change. Then, think what you could do to change it, something that is totally unfamiliar and maybe out of your comfort zone.

For example: You love sweets but know they are not good for your health. You know water is a necessity for good health so you decide to have a glass of water every time you think of having a sweet. This will deter you and flush the sugar out of your system. And every time you buy your groceries, you walk past the sweets. You ignore them or say to yourself with a smile on your face 'I do not need those any more, they will only poison my body.' Say 'I choose to be healthy and drink more water.' Form a new habit.

Remember the seeds you sow (your thoughts), fertilise and water, will grow. Your conscious (Thinking) mind sows the seeds, your subconscious mind can only grow the seed (Manifest what you are wanting) if you plant and continue to nurture and water it (Believe, accept and take action towards the changes you want to happen).

Your subconscious mind cannot reason like your conscious mind, it has to accept.

> *"View your mistakes as a learning curve.
> Mistakes are not a sign of incompetence.
> They are a sign of having made an attempt."*

What is a habit?

A habit is a behaviour that is repeated regularly and tends to occur subconsciously, in other words it has become familiar to and embedded in your mind and body. Or from a psychological stand point a habit is "a more or less fixed way of thinking, willing, or feeling, acquired through previous repetition of a mental experience."

When you understand how neural pathways are created in the brain, you can truly comprehend how you form habits and you can change and let them go.

When you form a neural pathway, you connect two nerve cells in the brain, which is called a synapse. Imagine each time you do this, you create a connection; you are creating a neuro-pathway that I relate to as a piece of string and each time you do the same thing, again and again, you add to the thickness of the string until it eventually resembles a rope. It gets thicker and thicker each time you repeat the same words or actions. This is creating a habit, the thicker the rope gets, the more entrenched the habit becomes, whether positive or negative.

Or, you could relate it to a super highway. Each time you travel over the same highway, it becomes more familiar, right? Well, that is how a habit is formed. Every time you do or say the same thing, the highway or neural pathway, becomes stronger, forming a pattern, a habit, a super highway.

The good news is, because of neuroplasticity, the brain's ever-changing potentials, anything is possible. You can break a pathway down and form new ones.

Research has shown that people who have had strokes can retrain their brains to function again by building new pathways. So, imagine what you can do by learning new behaviours and changing your attitude; you can transform your life.

Yes, smokers, addicts, overeaters; every one of you can learn new behaviours and attitudes and transform your lives. If you keep doing what you always have, you will continue to get the same results or, in many cases, dis-ease within your mind and body. You need to create new positive habits, actions and emotions, to create new neural pathways.

Another thing to remember is, when you want to change something, or are wanting something new in your life, always think of what it is you **want** not what you **don't want**, because where you place your thoughts, you also place your energy. Thoughts *are* energy. Many people keep focusing on what they don't want in their life, hence they create it. For example: if you want to attract a partner with certain qualities, write them down to affirm them and forget the qualities you don't want to attract.

Habits can be good or not so good. They will affect your health either way.

Most of the time, we don't even realise that we have formed a habit, that is how powerful and automatic your subconscious mind is, once it is programmed. The mind tells the body what to do without any effort on our behalf.

For example, many years ago, I used to smoke cigarettes (yuk), yes. I, too, wanted to be cool like many other teenagers. Every time I would pick up the phone to call someone, or the phone would ring, I would light a cigarette. Or if I sat down to a cup of coffee or a glass of wine I would light a cigarette. It was an automatic response; it was familiar, a habit. So, when I wanted to give up smoking, I needed to change my thoughts and actions, replace them with something new, like get a glass of water. The water served as a deterrent, plus it helped flush the nicotine, which was creating the addiction, out of my system.

It sends shivers down my spine now thinking of the unhealthy lifestyle I led many years ago. I was actually an expert at giving up, I did it many times. Once I learnt the power of the mind, it was much easier.

Many habits turn into addictions, such as; eating for comfort, taking drugs and or alcohol to numb something out of one's life. However, not all addictions start with a habit. Many addictions are formed through stress, or unpleasant experiences which could be from an event. A comment made during childhood or even as an adult, or through loneliness from the loss of a friend or partner. It then becomes a habit.

Here is an example of forming habits and programs within; as mentioned previously, if you travel over a superhighway (Neural pathway) many times the pathway becomes more and more familiar; it is ingrained.

Let's take driving for example; once you have driven a vehicle many times, it becomes second nature to you, right? For years you have been driving the same European car, you get in, put your foot on the clutch, turn the key. You know exactly what to do to start it, back it, and turn the wipers or lights on and off. No sweat, you've got it, right? Hello, you go on holiday and rent a car, a Japanese model. You go to put the key in to start it and there is no key, all you have to do is push a button. You put the blinker on to go around a corner or turn on the lights and the wipers start up instead. You finally get it right after a few days of repetitive driving and then your holiday ends. You get back into you own car and oops, you just turned the wipers on instead of the lights.

You had to learn new ways with the Japanese car, forming new pathways, habits. Now you have to reprogram yourself to go back to your own car. Luckily however, you have a strong neural pathway imbedded in your subconscious mind for driving the European car, so it doesn't take long to change back. This shows that one can fall back into old habits if not careful, so you need to really embed the new positive habit you are replacing it with.

Repetition is the name of the game. That is why I keep repeating *'the words you say and the pictures you create in your mind, create your reality,'* because I really want you to get it!

Here is another personal experience; I changed my car and even though both cars were Japanese, there are a few little differences like key and no key. But the one that has got me is, I had got so familiar with using cruise control in my previous car and don't have it now. When I get out on a highway, even 15 months later, I still want to put on cruise control to keep me from going over the speed limit. I so missed it; it was a good habit I had formed. I also have a heavy foot at times, especially when the road is clear and I don't like speeding tickets. I have had to form a habit of regularly checking my speed.

Habits are easily formed. You may be under stress in a relationship, or at work. You may have lost a friend or loved one. In situations like this, it is common to be upset and be in need of comforting. We all react differently to different circumstances and emotional times, not always positively. You may go to a specific food like chocolate or ice cream, reach for a cigarette or pour yourself coffee or a wine. If you do this for comfort when stressed over and over again, it forms a neural pathway within your brain, connecting an emotional situation or feeling with that food, drink or drugs, forming a habit or an addiction.

The hopeful fact however, as I said previously, is that the brain is always changing and you **can** forge new neuro pathways, creating new habits. You can replace not so good habits with good ones if you have a *Big Why*, the will to do so. It is never too late to change and there is help through agencies and holistic healers.

Habits can be good, like regular exercise, eating healthy food, whatever you do. If you put emotion with it, it will be stronger, staying in your mind.

> "Everything that's worthwhile in life comes to us free- our minds, our souls, our bodies, our hopes, our dreams, our intelligence, our love, our family, our friends and country. All of these priceless possessions are free."
>
> 'Earl Nightingale'

Change your habits, change your life.

If you have the knowledge and the will, you can build new neuro pathways to rewire or reprogram your brain. You can shrink, make redundant or better still, remove unhealthy behaviour, thoughts or addictions directly from the brain. Depending on the depth of the emotion, or the strength of the event that has led you to the habit or addiction, you may need help from a professional to get through it. There are many therapists, hypnotherapists, doctors and psychiatrists out there that can assist you, help you through times of stress. You do not have to do it alone. It is a matter of recognising that you need help early enough so as not to become addicted to a passive habit, get more stressed or create dis-ease within your mind or body. You can do it without pharmaceutical drugs. Don't fall into the trap of *'take another pill.'* Your brain is the most powerful drug you have.

There are many habits you can change once you are aware of them and decide to take responsibility for yourself and your behaviour. You can choose to take control of your own life, without drugs and therapists.

 First, you need to make sure you want to make changes. Realise the damage, if any, your stress levels, emotional ups and downs and or habits are doing to your health, your self-worth, self-esteem, your life. Then, and only then, can you take action that will be effective.

The following is an exercise you can do to help change a habit.

Write down-

> ➢ What habit you would like to transform, then answer the following:
>> o What is your big 'Why?' Why do you want to change?

- o How will you feel when you have changed?
- o What will be the benefits to your mind, body and life if you make these changes?
- ➢ Now write down all of the actions you can take that will help you make the changes you desire.
- ➢ Then, choose one or two of the action steps and give yourself a realistic timeframe for them.

It could be a great idea to get a friend or partner to do this with you. You can hold each other accountable.

Do not judge or be hard on yourself if you skip a day or two. If you start procrastinating, tell yourself that you chose to do this, as when you choose to do something it is easier to do.

One important thing you need to remember is that your mind likes what is familiar and it doesn't like unfamiliar. If left to its own devices, it will always want to go back to what is familiar; it will try to avoid what is unfamiliar. If you want success in changing a habit or succeeding in anything new, you have got to make what is familiar unfamiliar and what's unfamiliar, familiar. You have to really want to make those changes.

Think about it, if you start going to the gym, it will be a challenge and you will be stiff or sore the next day. Your body (through your thoughts) is going to say to you "to hell with this, I'm not used to it and it hurts, forget it". However, if you continue to go to the gym, it will become easier, familiar and even enjoyable and you will want to keep going. It will no longer be unfamiliar.

Here is an example of the exercise to get you started;

Q: What would I like to transform?

A: ***Mental and Physical Fitness Level***

Q: What is my big 'Why' Why do I want to change?

A: *To be slimmer and healthier and to be around longer for myself and my loved ones.*

Q: How will I feel when I have changed this habit?

A: *Fantastic, healthy, it will boost my pride, energy level, self-esteem and self-worth.*

Q: What will be the benefits?

A: *I will be able to do more, feel better and look better. I could even love myself.*

Actions I can take to help me achieve my goal:

Go for a brisk half hour walk at least five days a week.

Sign up to a gym (and use it), or take up Yoga, Qi Gong or Tai Chi

Meditate at least 10 minutes daily

Tell myself - I am getting fitter and healthier, say it several times a day

After two weeks, increase my walks to one hour and start introducing steps or hills, or buy a bike and start riding

You need to form good habits that will keep you healthy in mind and body.

I was taught by 'Roger Hamilton' many years ago that 'to know and not to do is not yet to know'. It made me think for a while. It means, if you realise and know that your actions or habit is detrimental to your health and you don't take action to remedy the situation, then you really don't know how detrimental it is to your health.

For example: If you know that smoking is not good for your health and you keep smoking, then you really don't know how bad it is for you; you haven't learnt yet. If you did and could visualise dying a slow death, not able to breathe, you would make the effort. Right?

If you knew how bad drinking excess alcohol was for your liver and your relationships, you would do something about it.

If you knew what taking drugs was doing to your brain and eating lots of sugary foods was doing to your mind and body; if you knew the consequences of continuing, you would take action to rectify it. You have choices and when you choose to do something, you are more likely to continue doing it and enjoy it.

Habits often have a bad reputation…but some habits can be helpful and healthy.

Think about what you would like to change in your life by creating healthy habits. Let's look at what a good habit might look like. Healthy eating, exercising regularly, giving your partner a hug and kiss before leaving the house and on return, taking a walk through nature at least once a week, turn your phone and TV off and read a good book more often. You can form a habit of doing any of these things, they are all good habits.

So, start replacing not so good habits with good habits. You can do it and you will feel so amazing when you do.

Do you procrastinate? Are you over weight? Do you talk too much and not listen? Are you unfit and need to exercise? Are you a smoker, take drugs or drink too much? Do you constantly grizzle about and concentrate on what is wrong? Have a *poor me, victim* mindset?

Think of what you could and would like to change and then start with small actions to make changes. We often try to jump in and make a major change too fast that is not always doable.

Actually, the words 'could' and 'should' need to be eradicated from your vocabulary. Just do it, without blame or making judgement, don't 'should' on yourself or others, and *could* has connotations of 'might or 'maybe'. Words like don't, not and no are also negatively orientated words. Try to tell your dog you are NOT going for a walk, what does it hear? All it hears is the word walk. 'Try' is another word to delete from your thoughts and vocabulary, don't try, just do it. If you say you are going to try something, there is an element of doubt that it could fail. 'If' is another word to be selective with. It is a big little word. If only I was, if only I had, if only I could.

Here's a good one, when you say I am trying to lose weight, guess what? When you lose something you always try to find it. So, if you want to reduce weight it is best not to say 'try' or 'lose'.

The above words are all a bit like ANT's, they need to be eradicated. Bring on the APT's (Automatic positive thoughts). I can, I will, I am happy, I am healthy and fit, I am donating my excess weight to the universe, I am enough- thin enough, clever enough, smart enough, loveable enough, I have phenomenal coping skills. Be positive and your life will change for the good.

> "Changing a mental habit requires a deliberate choice and takes dedication, time, and practice".
>
> 'Henry David Thoreau'

Fear

Most people resist change, they have a fear of what might be. Like I said earlier, your mind and body like what is familiar. As Dr Ulric Williams said; "No dis-ease is incurable, but some people are, because they don't want to change. They go down to death like a sheep in a slaughter race, just because they will not change."

Where your thoughts go, energy flows, so when you fear something, you are attracting it to you. The thoughts in our mind will fight what is unfamiliar if we are not open to change. Fear can set in.

Dealing with fear is not always easy, especially if we are not sure where it is coming from. We survive on the planet by avoiding pain, it is built into our DNA, dating back to the stone age. Our ancestors had to feel the fear and be aware of it to survive, or they would have been eaten by a lion, tiger or bitten by a snake.

We need a little fear to keep us safe. However, we also need to watch that fear is not holding us back with the what-ifs. We go to stroke a dog; it bites us, so we shy off going near dogs again, even though most dogs are friendly and wouldn't hurt a flea. Maybe that's not such a good example, as dogs do try to kill fleas, but you know what I mean. Sometimes we need to bite the bullet to move forward in life, to take chances. If you focus on something, you attract it, especially if you put emotion into the equation.

An example of this; If you focus on a pain, let's say a headache, it will get worse and then your emotions get involved, fear sets in, you think 'omg if I don't take something to kill this pain it will get worse'. You think you need a drug to kill the pain, which will only numb the pain, block the electrical signal in your brain; it won't get to the cause. It will most probably create another issue in your body.

You need to get into that filing cabinet, your subconscious mind, to the source where there will be a toxic thought or event that has triggered fear, and caused the headache, your pain and emotions. It could be self-criticism, fear.... too much going on, a food or drink, too much sugar, or lack of food or water (lack of water will cause dehydration, causing a headache). You need to get to the source and clear it. Actually, if you have a glass or two of water and do a bit of reflexology by rubbing the tips of your big toes, they will hurt; keep rubbing and your headache will go. You don't need a pill. We do create our lives and we can choose to change it.

Here is a true-life story of how fear can affect you. When she was very young, my aunty was chased by her brother who was holding a bird. Ever since that day, she has been scared of birds and even a feather. She would scream if anyone came near her with a feather. Can you imagine it? It stopped her from doing so many things for almost a life time. Birds and feathers are everywhere, in a park, on the beach, on clothing and hats. She was literally paranoid about them until one day, when in her eighties; she wanted to stay with her son in Australia. Her son had a caged bird which he loved. My aunty could not get away from being in the same room and was finally convinced that if it stayed in its cage it couldn't harm her. She was affected by that one event for over 75 years; she never got help to get over her fear.

The more we concentrate on something the bigger it gets, the more likely we are to attract it to ourselves. This is a Law of the Universe and you need to know how to control it so it doesn't manifest into what you don't want. Fair can affect you physically and mentally. It can affect your bladder and kidneys, that is why children and some adults wet themselves. Why many children wet their beds, fear of a parent, teacher or some other authority.

The good news is if we can and do attract negative and bad we can do the opposite, so doesn't it make sense that you do the opposite, turn your thinking around and attract positive things in your life. To stay at the extreme of fear is stagnation plus mental and physical deterioration.

So if you get bad news about your health, your relationship is stagnant or disruptive, you have sore knees, hips, back, whatever.... turn your thinking around, start concentrating on what you desire. This attitude will give you confidence and turn your life around.

The infinite power of your subconscious mind is always moving on your behalf, it does what you keep concentrating on, what you are telling it constantly. It will not fail you if you stay positive and tell yourself good things.

The things you fear do not really exist accept as thoughts in your mind. Thoughts are creative and will grow if given attention. Think good and good will follow.

Nothing can disturb you but your own thoughts. The suggestions, statements, or threats of others have no power over you. **The power is within you,** when you concentrate on the positive your life will change immensely.

So, think how you are thinking. If you need help, seek it. THINK POSITIVE, it will change your life. Do a check-up from the neck up regularly and be aware of your thoughts and words.

Avoid thinking or saying "I'm tired," "I'm hurt," "I'm angry". Instead, think and say, "I've chosen to be tired, hurt, or angry". Or better still, "I'm choosing to be happy". It's ok to be down every now and then; it is how long you choose to be down for that will affect your health.

You don't get "hit" by feelings. You feel them based on your perceptions. You perceive based on your beliefs, and you believe as you choose.

If you have fears, question them. Are they real? Where did they come from? Is it still relevant to have this fear?

You may be surprised at the answers and how you can turn the fear around.

Don't allow fear to hold you prisoner for a lifetime.

Here are a couple of acronyms for FEAR

Feel Excited and Ready

False Evidence Appearing Real

You are your words and thoughts!

"I have learnt that courage was not the absence of fear, but the triumph over it.
The brave man is not one who does not feel fear,
but he who conquers it".

'Nelson Mandela'

Chapter 5

Nothing Happens by Mistake, We Are Not Broken.

Your body can heal itself.. 80
Dis-ease must have a cause 84
Nothing can irritate you without your consent............................ 87
Your most destructive critic is you 90

"We are what we think.
All that we are arises with our thoughts.
With our thoughts, we make the world."

Buddha

Your body can heal itself

You too are a healer; we are all healers. I am convinced that every 'body' can heal itself given the right environment, state of mind and healthy thinking. There are so many people out there that have cured themselves of cancer, diabetes, addictions, joint pain plus much more without drugs and surgery. They just changed their mindset, their attitude and lifestyle. Where your mind goes, energy flows and vice-versa, so we need to think how we are thinking.

A few people I admire and have learnt from that have cured themselves are- Dr Fredrick Bailes, cured himself of Diabetes before insulin had been discovered, Louise Hayes cured herself of cancer, Chunyi Li Master of Spring forest Qi Gong cured himself of arthritis and severe suicidal depression and Energy Medicine Lady Donna Eden healed herself of multiple sclerosis. They all have amazing stories.

Ulric Williams, born in New Zealand in 1890, trained as a Doctor in Edinburgh and Cambridge Universities in 1918. He was a respected surgeon but became dissatisfied with surgery and drugs as a means of healing. He saw the body as such a marvellous creation and surgery seemed like mutilating it. Ulric became a doctor of Natural Therapy and set up 4 healing homes in Wanganui NZ in the 1930's. His story and many successful healing stories of his patients are told in the book 'New Zealand's Greatest Doctor', written by an ex patient named Brenda Sampson.

As a child, I used to get bronchitis. I remember being at the beach during the summer holidays and not being allowed to swim. Now when I get a cold, I know my body is telling me to slow down and start being selfish. To think of myself instead of everyone else. We just need to think how we are thinking at the time of discomfort and learn where our dis-ease is coming from. If we look after ourselves, find the cause, the thinking, our dis-ease can turn itself around. Feed the mind and body the right thoughts and foods; it works. Our bodies are designed to heal themselves.

However, as the old saying goes "You can take a horse to water but you can't make it drink"? As Dr Ulric Williams said; "There are no incurable dis-eases, only incurable people."

I have found the biggest issue with many people I speak to and work with, is lack of knowledge, not knowing the cause or what to do to turn it around. Or go onto Google and diagnose themselves instead of going within for the answers.

Secondly, there is often a lack of persistence, expecting instant results, forgetting that their dis-ease may have taken weeks, months or even years to manifest.

And thirdly is fear, mainly fear of veering away from the doctor's advice and taking the pills that have been prescribed to mask or numb the problem. I am not belittling doctors, although I don't go there myself, they do have their place, just as some medication and surgery does. But I find doctors very seldom seek the cause of an illness, they are so quick to give you a pill or cut it out. Nine times out of ten, both options lead to further complications, because most drugs are chemicals, foreign to our body.

Let's face it, what can anyone learn about you in a 10-minute appointment?

If you don't get to the root, find out and address what is causing your dis-ease, how are you going to cure the problem? It is likely to keep returning. It is not usually what's wrong that matters, it is why there is anything wrong. What is happening in your mind? To your emotions? How are you eating, living? What is happening in your relationships? If you sit quietly and ask yourself these questions, the answer will be there, most times you will know within yourself. Your subconscious mind knows.

Interestingly, surveys of over 130 US Medical schools show that doctors have on average only 23.9 hours of nutritional training in 4 years of training. Jennifer Barraclough, in her book 'Focus on Healing', a holistic self-help book for medical issues, says "Luckily many doctors are realising that there is a need to work holistically".

Does your doctor ask you about your relationships, the food you eat, how much and what sort of exercise you do, how much quality sleep you get, how much water you drink? Or make any recommendations on any of the above, instead of giving pills? If so, great. If not, don't go back; find another doctor or health therapist.

Everyone needs to take some responsibility for their own health. Don't let fear take over. When given a scary diagnosis, I know it is frightening and you often go into 'fight or flight' mode. If you take action in this mode you are likely to make the wrong decision. Ask questions, delay treatment, to make your own decision. You have time to read and research, you have options. In saying that, check that the information you are reading is well founded. Don't allow people, family and friends with little knowledge and more than likely are talking out of fear because they love you, social media or doctors, to scare you into the wrong decisions. Use your gut instinct, your intuition.

Your body was designed to heal itself, given the right conditions. Everybody is a healer; you can heal your mind and body; you just need to learn how. I want to help you on your journey to happy, healthy living. An unbalanced mind, body, and spirit creates dis–ease within, which in turn will show up as minor or major health problems – Heart, Skin, Joints, Organs, Mind...... As Marisa Peer, Rapid Transformational therapist and psychiatrist says

'A hurt that cannot cry will make an organ weep'.

If your mind and body can create dis-ease, it can also cure it.

When you learn to take responsibility for your own life, to love and nurture your whole self, life is amazing. You CAN do it; you are a healer. YOU can heal yourself - mind, body and spirit. Believe it, live it, love yourself and start living free of pain; both physical and emotional. Living love, joy, peace, gratitude and happiness, will lead to a more blissful happier life. So, don't wallow in self-pity, know that your body can heal itself, take responsibility for your situation and life and change what you can. When you change the input, you change the outcome.

"To heal means 'make whole'. A person torn apart by his/her fear, hates, greed's, is not a whole person. He /she is a circle with one or more segments missing"

'Dr. Frederick Bailes'

Dis-ease must have a Cause

You are a winner. You were the winning sperm that joined the egg, creating you. We all started life by an egg and a sperm coming together – They become one cell, then multiply from 1 to 2 – 4- 8 to 50 trillion cells and during the course of a lifetime you get a cut, a burn, a break, a virus and your body heals itself, it is a normal process.

There is no mistake, **a dis-ease must have a cause**, it's the body reacting to surrounding elements, the stress you perceive. *Rob Overbruggen, (PHD Meta Meditation)*

We don't have to tell our heart how to beat and make our blood flow through our veins, our lungs how to breathe, our digestive system how to work, our lymphatic system to cleanse our blood and tissues, or a bone how to heal. Our deeper mind knows and is keeping it all going without any conscious effort from our surface or conscious mind. It is contracting muscles so we can take a walk, play a piano, or scratch our self. We don't know and don't consciously need to know how it all works. It will happen automatically if we choose to allow our body to be natural and healthy. Just like we don't need to know how power gets to a light bulb when we turn on a light switch, or how we can see and talk to people on the other side of the world.

There's nothing that happens by mistake, we are not broken or missing anything when we come onto this earth. Every time we experience a so called problem in our body, it is a doorway to see what our symptoms are to access this invisible, unseen energy that guides our cells to communicate from our brain, to our body, to the outside world, so that we can adapt at any given moment.

When you can begin to look at symptoms such as; addictions, pain, stress and depression as the underlying cause of everything that keeps you unhappy and in pain and realize it all derives from past emotional experiences, trapped emotions or emotional baggage; you can start to deal with them. You need to monitor the recurring pictures from those past events that you are creating in your mind and the words you are continually saying to yourself. Do your regular check up from the neck up, be aware of what is happening, reoccurring in your mind.

Things happen, life happens, we break a leg, get a cold, whatever happens, happens for a reason. It is telling us there's something we need to be aware of. If something you perceive as bad happens, it has happened for a reason. There are lessons to be learnt from it. How you react to and perceive everything that happens to you determines the outcome, your reality.

I had an elderly client that fell and broke her leg. I asked her if she had been asking for a break. 'I sure have' she said and away she went, raving on about how she had been asking her husband to take her on holiday for 10 years and he kept making excuses why they couldn't. Then all of a sudden, she stopped, looked at the expression on my face and said, 'oh my goodness, I have created this haven't I? I kept asking for a break.' I just nodded my head with a smile on my face.

I have asked the same question of many people that I have come across with a leg or arm in plaster, sure as eggs they have an aha moment, either saying OMG I have created this or they stop and think with a look on their face that says 'you are right. I have needed a break'.

I was talking to a mother of a child that didn't want to participate in his school sports day. She said he climbed a tree that morning, fell out and broke his arm. He was a very happy boy because he didn't have to participate in the sports.

The words you say to yourself and the pictures you create in your mind, create your reality. Yes, I am repeating myself again, and will continue to do so, as you know by now that we learn from repetition and these are the most important words I want you to grasp hold of. Your MIND is the key to healing your body. If you are thinking right, you will be living right, healthily. Life is a mirror and will reflect back what you put out there.

Teenagers are a good example. Everyone puts the pimply faces down to hormones. Next time you see a teenager with a few pimples, ask them who they are mad with, or angry at. Nine times out of ten they will tell you; mum, dad, my friend, teacher.... Pimples are little outbursts of anger. Another is a urinary tract infection. If you get one, reflect on who you are pissed off with. A hip problem is concerns about moving forward in life, many when approaching retirement get sore hips. A sore back is generally a lack of support, shoulder problems are usually carrying the world on your shoulders, frozen shoulder is where you don't want to be where you are, you are feeling stuck. Alzheimer's is when you want to escape from the world.... People who are constantly angry, end up with liver problems; they often have bad breath and swear a lot.

At the end of the day, every thing is Energy, including words and pain; we are all Energy. Our bodies are very intelligent. They can heal themselves if given the right environment – Good positive energy, healthy eating, exercise, relationships, activities, workplace and most importantly, healthy thinking. Oh, my goodness, did I repeat myself? I sure did, because your thinking is the number one creation of your reality, it is worth repeating.

> "Be careful of your thoughts, they may become words at any moment."
>
> 'Lara Gassen'

Nothing can irritate you without your Consent

Many cannot grasp that experiences in themselves have no power to irritate them. They get so bogged down with the event, how someone made them feel, who was to blame, or how it happened, they go on and on giving it more energy. This increases the energy of the experience, making it bigger, keeping it growing and festering.

I have done it myself in the past, with people who have tried to belittle me many years ago when I was in politics, or butted in on conversations when others are talking, I allowed them to irritate me. When I finally realised that life is a mirror, it reflects what you are putting out there, it was a revelation.

So, when people irritate you, think about it. Are they reflecting what is in you? It was for me. I have learnt that it is rude to butt in on others' conversations, even if I have something important to say. If you don't remember what you were going to say, then maybe it wasn't meant to be said at that time.

I have also learnt that the only one I can change is myself, my attitude towards others, and I need to accept them for who they are. It doesn't mean that I have to agree with or like what they say or do. I just had to realise that that was their way, their opinion, and I can't change them, but I can change myself so those reflections wouldn't come back to me. From that day on, it has been much easier to accept situations if I can't avoid them. I have learnt that the best way to deal with situations I am not agreeable with or, are in my eyes is rude, was to just let it go over my head and not take what they said or did to heart. I reject it so it doesn't embed itself into my subconscious mind, my filing cabinet.

A suggestion from others has no power over you except the power you give them through your own thoughts. You have to give your mental consent; you have to entertain the thought. Then it becomes your thought and you do the thinking. Remember, you have the capacity to choose. Choose what you want to accept, choose love and health.

It is our reaction to the experience or suggestion that irritates us, e.g. One person will love a yellow car and another will hate it; one person believes purple and red go well together; another will see these colours together repulsive. One person will love rock music, it will irritate another.

Night time is a good example. When you are trying to sleep, there might be a party in the street, your partner may be snoring, a dog barking or a tap dripping that you can't stop. Water dripping will irritate one person; even enrage them if it is consistent, while another may imagine listening to falling rain putting them to sleep. If your partner is snoring you have options; you could try to roll them over, wake them and ask them to turn over, or, just like the party down the road, pretend they are playing music to put you to sleep. Or you could just lie there and get irritated. You have choices.

Someone's loud or shrieking laugh will irritate one person while another will think it is fun and it makes them happy to hear it. If there were some irritating qualities in colours, loud music, a dripping tap or a laugh, it would irritate everyone equally; therefore, the irritation arises within you and is your reaction to something neutral.

This relates to the use of one of your mind power abilities talked about previously, 'perception', it is all about how you perceive and react to everything. To me, it makes sense to look for the good in everything and everyone, and respond appropriately.

Other sources of irritation may be members of your family, friends, work colleagues, financial worries or some environment you are not happy with. It could be any number of external experiences, an irritation from the external world, or even yourself.

How often do you get irritated with yourself?

As previously said, we all have choices – You can allow something or someone to irritate you constantly, which will in turn create discomfort, misery or dis-ease, or you can recognise that it just is what it is and let it go and remain free from irritation and dis-ease.

Oh, and remember irritation with someone or something often causes an itch or rash. So, monitor your thinking and reactions.

"If you can change your mind, you can change your life."

'William James'

Your most destructive critic is you

Did you realise that you are harder on yourself than anyone else? Think about how you talk to yourself at times. I'm too fat, too skinny, not good-looking enough, I have too many wrinkles, I'm stupid, lazy, not good enough, etc etc etc, and on it goes. Have you ever done something you perceive silly and then said 'oh, you stupid idiot', or 'omg, why do I always do this or that'? It's stupid of me. Or think of the images you create in your mind that disturb and upset you, you replay a past event that you aren't proud of and continually put yourself down for it. Think of the habits you may have formed for comfort, or to numb pain in your mind or body, smoking, drinking too many coffees. These are all destructive and create dis-ease.

If friends spoke to you, or treated you as you treat yourself at times, would they still be your friends?

Always remember that the past is in the past; it is gone. Tomorrow is a mystery. Who knows what will happen tomorrow and today is the present, a gift. So be aware, consciously live in the present and start making changes for the good, take responsibly for your life and enjoy it. Be selfish, but in a good way.

Do you consider yourself selfless or selfish? You often hear people call others selfish or selfless. Selfish in most people's minds has negative connotations, meaning only thinking of self. Well I say go for it, be selfish, you need to be number one in your life. If you don't, or can't look after yourself, how can you be fit and healthy enough to look after others or expect others to look after you?

Too often I have come across clients that have been selfless. They have been so busy running after others and forgetting their own needs, they have drained themselves, or let others drain them. Yes, they end up needing help.

When you love, respect and care for yourself you will have excess love to give and will receive love from others in abundance. Love and look after yourself first, it is not selfish, it is good, be selfish. I am. It took me a long time to learn this lesson.

Kick those thoughts that others will think you are selfish, choose to replace them with good healthy habits so you can live, love and be loved longer. Always remember, you can only change yourself, you cannot control what others choose to think and do. When you change yourself others will notice and hopefully follow, be a leader and your life will change for the good.

Always remember you have an amazing powerful mind and it does what it thinks you want, what you continually tell it. When it gathers up new information of what you are seeing, smelling, tasting, hearing, feeling, experiencing, your mind is creating new emotions, new neural pathways and experiences.

It will feel unfamiliar to start with and your body and mind may even say to you 'this isn't right, I am being selfish, forget it'. Don't listen to it, as the more you continue with your good habits, they will become familiar and habitual. Your life will transform and others will notice, comment and love you for it because you will be a happier, healthier person.

"At the age of 18, I made up my mind to never have another bad day in my life. I dove into an endless sea of gratitude from which I've never emerged."

'Patch Adams'

PART 2

Solutions for Healthy Living

Take Control of Your Power, Your Life.. 93
Self-Esteem 118
Control Your Stress, Change Your Life... 138
Food – Good or Bad?.. 152
Life Force Energy 173
Relationships.. 213
Music and Meditation 223
Sleep 235
Muscle Testing... 244
Exercises and Remedies... 252

Take Control of Your Power, Your Life

Are you reliving the past?.. 94
Forgiveness and letting go.. 97
Healthy thinking is paramount 102
Emotions and feelings 108
The rise and fall of thoughts 112
Thoughts with feelings strengthen the outcome 115

"Very little is needed to make a happy life;
It is all within yourself, in your way of thinking."

Marcus Aurelius

Are you reliving the past?

There are people so confused because they think they are living healthy lives. They are drinking plenty of water, exercising, eating healthily, meditating and yet they still experience dis-ease, of the Heart, Cancer, or Allergies. Why?

At the core of it all are emotions and energies buried in the subconscious mind, limiting beliefs from past events. Memories have a big impact on your life and can even be debilitating if not recognised and dealt with. Your mind should be your best friend, but for too many of us, our mind is our own worst enemy. We allow it to keep getting in our way. The good news is that you can change it.

Humans are the only living thing on the planet that choose to relive painful events over and over again by replaying them in their heads. The single biggest cause of dis-ease is your past; emotional, trapped baggage. Animals let it go. A gazelle can be chased by a lion and 30mins later it is grazing peacefully. We, however, hang onto it.

What you replay in your mind will dictate the kind of emotional state you live in. As I have previously stressed, your mind is so very powerful. Dwelling on the past, holding onto events consciously or unconsciously only leads to an unhappy life; full of bitterness, resentment, self-pity, and stress. Why? Because the body doesn't know the difference between an event that is taking place in your outer world and an event you are creating or recreating by thought alone.

A life that is consumed by bitterness and resentment is hardly a life worth living. When anger and resentment consume you, this only leads to depression and a life of misery, where you feel a victim and powerless.

So, if you want to improve the state of your being, become aware of the stories you are playing in your mind. You can choose the life you want to create, but before you can do that, it is important to let go of the past.

Not only do we hold onto memories in our minds, but our bodies also hold onto memories, and when this happens, dis-ease can show up in different organs and parts of the body. It could appear in reoccurring back, hip or knee problems.

Back in 2008, I had grinding hips when I walked and pain lying in bed. I would lie on one side and it would ache so I would turn over, only to have the other side ache. I thought I was going to have to have a hip replacement. However, I found out those sore hips were all about moving forward in life, our legs and hips carry us forward. I was worried about the future. In other words, I was creating pictures in my mind of what might or might not happen, the big 'IF' stories we all create, what if this happens or doesn't happen.

When I realised what I was doing to myself, my hips came right, the magnificent mind-body healing happened automatically. So, every time I get a twinge in a hip now, I do a check-up from the neck up, think how I am thinking and the pain disappears.

Our mind-body connection is amazing. Another example is skin irritations; your skin is your largest organ and if you are irritated, frustrated, annoyed with someone or something, it can show up as an itch or rash and you start scratching. If left without checking your thinking, it will grow and you could end up continually scratching and creating a rash, psoriasis or some other skin irritation. Be careful, because if you get really pee'd off with someone, you could end up with a urinary tract infection, or if angry, remember pimples are little outbursts of anger and could appear.

Your body, I call it nature, is amazing, so look after it and it will look after you. Your body is designed to be healthy, to heal itself; it is your mind that you need to keep in check, as that is what takes you off track.

It is amazing how the entirety of living deliberately, on purpose, can be summed up in just three words- *'Thoughts become things.'*

Of course, beliefs are important too, but your thoughts can change what you believe.

Words are also important; they are your thoughts that will become things the soonest.

And taking action is absolutely critical because it alone connects the dots.

"When you can't control what's happening, challenge yourself to control the way you respond to what's happening. That is where your power is"

'Buddha'

Forgiveness and letting go

Dwelling on past events is like taking poison! Stop poisoning your mind and body!

Forgiveness and letting go frees you – it frees you to live without the weight of anger and resentment. Forgiveness of others, and yourself, for the wrongdoings you have caused yourself or have suffered because of someone else's actions, has tremendous physical and psychological effects. Forgiveness of yourself and others leads to increased feelings of self-worth, self-esteem and decreases psychological stress. Let go of any hurt, so it no longer irritates you; when you let it go that person no longer has a hold on you.

In essence, they most probably have forgotten the event and have no idea that you are still holding onto it, screwing up your life. When you forgive yourself and others, it allows you to build your self-esteem, to live a more satisfied and fulfilling life, because you have decluttered your mind, moved beyond debilitating, negative thoughts, feelings and behaviour that keep you stuck and unhealthy.

'Knots of Resentment'

We have all held grudges at some time or another, both big and small. When you initially start out the practice of forgiveness daily, at first you might think you will run out of people to forgive or to ask forgiveness from. But it turns out that it is an ongoing process.

Here is a practice:

Close your eyes and visualize the person who wronged you or who you wronged.

Ask for forgiveness and then forgive them.

When you forgive, you may experience heat and vibration right under your heart, near your stomach, a gut feeling. It may feel like a knot has been untied. The more knots you untie, the more freedom you will experience. These knots are not needed; they cause blockages of energy flow and of breath. It takes psychic energy to hold a grudge. Forgive everyone for everything. Why would you want to hold onto negative energy? Let the energy flow easily through you!

Resentment causes knots that obstruct the flow of your energy, causing blockages and dis-ease. Forgiveness releases the knots to allow your energy to flow freely.

Just think of a river being dammed, image the build-up of water, logs and debris.

Now open the flood gates and see the water flowing freely.

'Be a victor, not a victim'

If you do it, feel it and mean it, letting go of the past will feel so good and it will give you much relief.

Earlier, I talked about the limiting beliefs that are holding us back and how we hold onto events in our subconscious mind.

Throughout our lives, we go through different experiences, some are positive and some we see as negative and unpleasant. When you hang on to a negative or unpleasant experience, you are constantly thinking about it, or your memory is triggered by something you see, hear, smell, taste or touch. Something you experience reminds you and brings back feelings and emotions that you would prefer not to have.

How many pleasant memories do you recall every day? Unfortunately, most people tend to remember the negative far more easily than remembering the positive and we hold onto it. These memories prevent you from moving forward and healing; let them go.

We are human, *we all make mistakes* – whether or not we want to admit to our mistakes is another thing entirely! When it comes to forgiveness, many of us would rather hold on to our hurts, our resentments and anger than forgive the one who has done us wrong. It takes a "bigger" person to forgive; someone who realises that holding on to all those negative emotions is only hurting *themselves; not* the person who committed the wrongdoing! Many times, that "other" person doesn't even know that they have hurt you or they have moved on, have forgotten all about the incident. They don't know, or at times even care that you are still holding onto it, still hurting (yourself).

We tend to think of forgiveness as only beneficial to the one who is guilty of the wrongdoing. When you forgive, it is so empowering; the one who is forgiven is also relieved. You can both go on with your lives, free. The other person doesn't need to know when you are forgiving them. When forgiving, you just need to say it out loud to yourself and mean it, you don't have to face them to forgive. So, let go of past grievances and memories that are not serving you in your current life. You can't look backwards and get ahead.

There is nothing you can do to change the past, except for in your mind, your memories, and the pictures you create of the event. So, forgive, forget and move on.

Forgiveness is really a gift that you give to yourself. It has very little to do with the person who has hurt you. It doesn't mean that you have to agree with, or condone, any wrong doing, whatever was said or done, or whoever it was that has impacted your life negatively. But if you forgive yourself and/or anyone else, you will declutter and clear your mind and you will move forward in life.

Holding onto grief and grievances to your body, is like taking poison. I say no more!

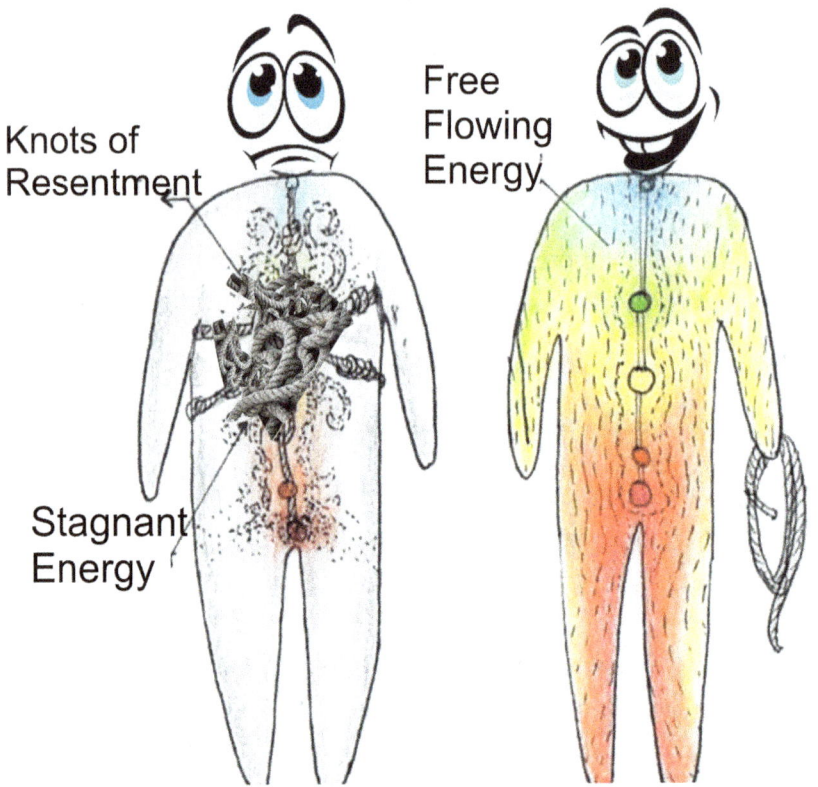

Affirmations to help let go and forgive

A best time for affirmations is first thing in the morning while you are still in that semi-sleep zone and/or as you are relaxing and going to sleep at night. This is when your subconscious mind best absorbs what you are telling it. I have mentioned earlier that your mind and body believe and do what you continually tell it to, especially if you add feelings and emotions to what you are affirming.

So, program your mind for how you want to be, do and have.

Use whatever affirmations resonate with you.

I am positive	I let go	I am forgiving
Life is wonderful	I am appreciative	I live in peace
I am well balanced	I see the good in all	I am confident
Now is all there is	I live in the now	I live in harmony
I am amazing	I am accepting	I am sharing
I am accepting	I am grateful	I allow
I am wise	I am whole	I am enough
I am fantastic	I am free of fear	I am free of anger
I am full of joy	I am happy	I laugh a lot
I am powerful	I am loved	I am loving
I am caring	I have all I need now	Life is a miracle
I give and receive	Good exists in all	I am in control
I am free of addictions	I release unwanted energy	I love unconditionally
I have a sense of humour	I believe in myself	I share smiles with everyone
I give and receive hugs freely		Everything comes to me as I need it
I am the only authority in my life		I am open to the spiritual world
I am one with the universe (God)		

"The first to apologise is the bravest.
The first to forgive is the strongest.
The first to forget is the happiest."

'Unknown author'

Healthy thinking is paramount.

The mind is like a battery, if you don't keep charging it with positive energy it will run flat and slowly die.

Self-care is so important, to feel and listen to your body. If you feel out of sorts, you feel there is something wrong, any discomfort or dis-ease within, it's your body letting you know that there is something wrong.

A few years ago, I had a client come to me with Vertigo; straight away I asked him what was happening in his life, he was overloaded at work, no surprise. His work life was unbalanced, work kept pouring in, he didn't know how to say no to a job and couldn't prioritise the work. Hence, he was going around in circles; he had manifested vertigo which was his mind and body saying "hey things aren't right". When I spoke to him a week later, he was so proud of himself, he had made changes, and he started to be honest with himself and his customers. He acknowledged that he couldn't keep everyone happy and do too many things at once. He told customers that he had many jobs booked and it would be at least a week before he could get to theirs. He prioritised and his health recovered, along with his confidence and self-esteem.

I mentioned my hip problem earlier, I just needed to do a check-up from the neck up, be aware of my thinking. As I said, my hip is fine now; if I get a twinge, which is very rare these days, I check my thinking and correct it. It is a pity that so many people don't realise that they can be a victor. They do not have to stay a victim; you can control your body and pain 99% of the time. Most people leave it too late, or they think it is too late, so it's off to the doctor for pills or the knife. It is so sad because, with the right environment, mindset, and care, your body can heal itself. If you can create it, you can cure it, just get to the cause and change it.

There are exercises you can do to relieve sore hips. See No.21 of the daily routine in Exercises and Remedies.

Another real-life story: *I had a friend, we will call him AB. AB had a sore hip, just like I did. He felt the pain and grinding when walking, and it ached when lying down. I used my pendulum on him and it told me that his hip was okay, there was nothing wrong with it. I told him to stop worrying about the future. I was aware of his current situation and guessed that he would be subconsciously concerned about where to from here, although he didn't show it externally. He didn't believe me and swore black and blue that he needed a hip operation. He decided to go to the doctors to have an x-ray, only to be told there was nothing wrong with his hip. When next I saw him, he said 'you were right', he finally decided to check his thoughts and lifestyle and is now cured, no operation. Keep in mind that if he didn't change his thinking and do the right exercises, he would more than likely have needed an operation eventually.*

This is happening everywhere and we need to help people to be aware of what they are doing to themselves that is affecting their health. And nine times out of ten can be avoided.

Listen to your body, it talks to you all of the time, whether it is pain, a break, sore abdomen, diarrhoea, an infection, rash, headache, cancer, heart attack, stroke, Alzheimer's, arthritis. You name it; you have more than likely created it. I know it is a hard pill to swallow, but it is true and when you get it early enough and sort it, it becomes the easiest pill to swallow that does not harm your body. So often, surgical intervention will cause further complications and I don't need to mention what pills can do to your body!!

Always remember you are "NUMBER ONE" in your life. First, you need to look after you, then and only then, you will have a healthy mind and body that will enable you to love yourself, and in turn love and help others. If you can't look after yourself, you won't have the right energy to look after and love yourself, let alone anyone else, and if you don't care for and look after yourself, how can you expect others to love or look after you? When you look after yourself, you feel good about yourself and life is so much more rewarding. Be selfish in a good way, think of number one first, 'you.'

Healthy thinking is so paramount. Every one of us has a different temperament and we react differently to life's challenges based on impressions embedded in our subconscious mind from past experiences, programming, and perceptions. Unfortunately, so many people just can't seem to shake negative thinking when it comes to certain situations, people, thoughts, and feelings and it has an effect on their whole life. We need to learn how to deal with and let it go.

Here are a few good examples of what people are affected by:

You may have been told when you were a child or young adult that you were hopeless, fat, weak, stupid. You may have had a bad experience in front of the class at school, or have been physically or mentally abused. Any of these can cause ongoing mental issues; you have started to stutter because you were continually told to "Shut up", you were too frightened to speak or got a major fright. This could also lead to you biting your nails, because you needed comfort or you were scared.

Whatever or however you were affected, it will more than likely be stopping you in your tracks when you try to do certain things, holding you back in life.

Another example; if you almost drowned at the beach as a child, you may fear the sea now and be missing all of those great sunny days enjoying the ocean and swimming in the surf with friends, all because of that one experience as a child. If your teacher or a relative told you that you will never be any good at anything, you will either be busting yourself trying to prove yourself or holding yourself back with the belief that you can't. Like my aunty in her 80's that feared birds, even feathers all of her life, all because she was chased by a relative with a bird in hand when she was little.

I had a client in her 80's who had had back problems all of her life. I helped her to relieve her pain with energy healing often, for many years, but the pain would come back after some time. When I used Rapid Transformation Therapy with her, we found out her problem went back to the day she was born. Her mother wanted a boy and didn't want anything to do with her, she was even named after the nurse that looked after her for some time. Throughout her life, her mother was never supportive, she felt second best to her sister. Her first husband left her for a younger woman, her second husband was verbally abusive, her daughter never supported her and her supportive son lived in another country and passed away in his 50's. She lived well, ate healthily, was very active in the community, meditated and was a successful businesswoman. Her back problems all came down to feeling a lack of support. The proof in the pudding was; she met an amazingly-supportive man, her soul mate, who came into her life for a few short years, transforming her considerably. Her back was so much better; she was in love and feeling happy and healthy. Unfortunately, he passed away and her back problems returned from a real or perceived lack of support.

Another true story is about a client was continually sabotaging her efforts to lose weight. Every diet she tried, she would lose so much weight then just stop; she could never get lower than a certain weight. When I worked with her, it was revealed that she was sexually abused as a child, in two separate households. I asked her if she was a pretty young girl, she said yes very pretty. It turned out that she was blocking herself from losing weight so that she would not be attractive and subjected herself to further abuse. What a realisation. She shocked herself when she understood what she was doing to herself. Understanding is so powerful, when you understand why you do what you do, what the underlying cause is, you can then deal with it.

We can hold ourselves prisoner for a lifetime through unhealthy thinking or buried issues deep in our subconscious mind. No matter how many pills you take, or operations you have, your problem will often come back if you don't find out the cause of your dis-ease and deal with it. Get help.

When you combine the two, 'healthy living and healthy thinking', where you have a strategy to get into these core emotions to shift them; you can transform your life.

We learnt how to release Knots of resentment however there a few other knot's you may need to release. Here is a prayer to help you release 'Knots in Your Life.'

Please give me the power strength and wisdom to:

Untie knots that are in my mind, heart and life.

Remove the have not's, the can not's and the do not's that I have in my mind

Erase the will not's and might not's that may have found a home in my heart.

Release me from the could not's, would not's and should not's that obstruct my life.

And most of all, dear universe, I ask that you remove from my mind, my heart and life all of the "AM NOT'S" that I have allowed to hold me back, especially the though that I am not GOOD ENOUGH.

"Keep your thought positive because it becomes your word.
Your word positive because it becomes your behaviour.
Your behaviour positive because it becomes your habits.
Your habit positive because it becomes your value.
Your value positive because it becomes your destiny".

'Mahatma Gandhi.'

Emotions and feelings

Emotions are Energy in Motion – Energy Movement

We are all beings of pure energy and we all have emotions.

Is there a difference between feelings and emotions? You can observe your feelings but not your emotions. You could say that emotions are much deeper and stronger than feelings. From one viewpoint, that's true.

When you experience feelings, you are in full control. You are the observer. It has been said that when you experience emotions, you cannot remain the observer and you are not in control, the emotion takes over. I believe that we can take control; it is just harder to when you are very emotional.

As soon as you take control and become aware of your emotions, they turn into feelings and thoughts, either positive or negative. Always remember that your thoughts turn into feelings and feelings turn into actions, which in turn creates your results in life.

Let's take a look at emotions.

Imagine you are watching a movie. One minute you could be splitting your sides laughing and the next minute something sad comes up and tears run down your face. Then, you could be watching something erotic and it will arouse you, or someone does or says something that may make you angry. Yes, we can switch from one emotion to another and we all have choices. We can suppress an emotion if need be, although it is not always good to do so.

Emotions appear to have a life of their own, one dictionary says 'emotions are a strong feeling deriving from one's circumstances, mood, or relationships with others, an instinctive or intuitive feeling as distinguished from reasoning or knowledge'. Another definition is 'the affective aspect of consciousness, a state of feeling, a conscious mental reaction (such as anger or fear) subjectively experienced as strong feelings usually directed toward a specific object and typically accompanied by physiological and behavioural changes in the body. This confirms my belief in emotions turning into feelings.

In most cases, you can only experience emotions and not control them. Your emotions are usually in control! That's the reason why we have emotional reactions to things that we sometimes later regret. We may yell at or say nasty things to our partner or children, say and do things we don't really mean and regret later. We argue with friends, and some throw and smash things. Mostly, an emotional state is reactive, uncontrollable, and seemingly independent from our core selves.

I love the saying: **"Put your brain into gear before you open your mouth"**. This is a great way to control emotions and save face in some situations. You are not so likely to 'put your foot in it' so to speak.

It is not all bad though; emotions can be very positive and deep. In a romantic situation, the love between partners, parent and child, friendships, pets, loved possessions are all positive relationships. All of these emotions can also lead to uncontrollable actions or reactions, physical or emotional when subjected to different circumstances. Feelings can also be physical or emotional especially those influenced by other people.

Being in a state of awareness is a great habit to create, be aware of thoughts, feelings, and emotions and it will change your life. You may think 'how is awareness a habit'? Surprisingly, most people are too busy doing instead of being, we are human beings, and most often not aware of what is going on in our mind and bodies. So, we need to make it a habit to be aware. When you become aware of and feel emotion, energies feel different and they can be changed with your thoughts.

The Vibrational Energy of Anger is a different vibration to that of Frustration or Sadness. All of these vibrations, emotions, stress your body. The core of every stress, symptom, and dis-ease is emotions, memories and traumatic perceptions that are buried in your subconscious mind

Trapped emotions stress your body, it distorts and irritates your energy field and body tissue and can cause cancer, increased heart rate, anxiety, depression, and many other dis-eases. Anger is stored in the liver, have you heard the old saying – 'He/she has a shitty liver' (Angry) Worry plays havoc with your spleen, pancreas and stomach. Anxiety affects your heart, nervous system and small intestines; frustration and anger affect your liver; depression and grief affect your colon and lungs which in turn slows down your immune system. Look after yourself, be aware of your reoccurring, unhealthy emotions and release them.

You both give and receive energy; you are affected by the energies of others around you and your energy affects others. I learnt about entrainment (Becoming in tune with or synchronised) when studying Quantum Touch healing. I learnt how to raise my energy high enough not to allow others to drain me and to allow others to entrain, bring their energy up to mine. This way they heal themselves. When your energy is low it is hard to heal, when it is raised your body can heal itself.

You entrain to your environment whether it is through being in nature, listening to music, the language and moods of those around you. Hence my advice would be if you don't like the vibrations and energy of those around you, move away.

Music is a great example– If you want to be relaxed put on soft background meditative music while you read a book. If you want to be energised play energising music, get up and dance or sing with it, get that feel good feeling.

Remember that your mood and energy affect those around you.

Be Happy, Keep Smiling.

"The removal of stress creates HEALTH"

"We can't solve problems by using the same kind of energy we used to create them"

'Albert Einstein'

The rise and fall of thoughts

If your thoughts can *make* you sick, they can also *heal* you!

Your body does not know the difference between a real or an imagined event. We create our lives by the pictures we create in our minds and the words we say to ourselves. Yes, I am repeating this important message.

Living in a negative emotion affects your whole body and sadly many people live in an emergency mode which is low energy, feelings of anger, hatred, anxiety, aggression, envy, insecurity, prejudice, fear, hopelessness, depression, powerlessness. These all have long term effects on your mind and body, let alone the people around you.

The good thing is – 'If our thoughts can make us sick, they can also heal us'. So why not live in peace, love, joy, happiness, security, high energy, gratitude, forgiveness.

As we just discussed, stored emotions are a record of the past. So, if emotion is stored in the body then the body is living in the past and the body is a major part of your unconscious mind and believes it is in the same conditions.

I lost my Grandmother in 1979, my father passed away in 1988and my sister in 2000. Funerals became a very emotional time for me after their passing and I tried to avoid them. Even hearing the song "Amazing Grace", which was played at theirs and almost every funeral I attended afterward, would set the tears and emotions flowing. The song triggered the emotions of my loss and sadness related to their death, it was embedded in my subconscious mind. When my sister passed away in 2000, I had to change my thinking; I had to be strong for her children and family. She had asked me to take her body to her home when she passed and be there to help her children through their grief; I told her I would see them through it. I had a mind shift, I had to be strong.

All of a sudden, I realised what I had been putting myself through for so many years. I even got very emotional at funerals of people I barely knew, I was just there for a friend, I didn't even know their relative.

I knew I had to change my perception of funerals, to realise the person who had passed would not want me to grieve forever, they would want me to be grateful that they were at peace and had been in my life, knowing that they will always be with me in my heart, mind, and spirit and we will all be there one day. Now I am a funeral celebrant and have helped many people through the loss of loved ones.

We tend to build up and hold onto thoughts and emotions because we have been taught to push them away or we don't want to feel or deal with things that don't feel good. Too often we look for answers outside of ourselves instead of inside, usually blaming others or life circumstances, forgetting or not realising that we create our reality. Men, in particular, think it is not macho to show emotions, in particular, cry. If the mind doesn't weep, the body will; we need to let it out to avoid dis-ease.

When our energy is trapped, we keep creating and repeating the same experiences. Too often we keep focusing on what we don't want rather than what we do want. The subconscious mind holds the key, the why, the real reason a person has dis-ease in their mind or body. If you are stuck, a good Therapist, healer or hypnotherapist can get to the core and help you to turn your life around.

From conception to the age of seven your subconscious mind is being programmed, coded with memories and emotional experiences. These memories have been filed away, stored in your subconscious mind and now create your belief system. Of course, from seven on, you have continued to have experiences that have also been filed away, however those early years are crucial. Those experiences and memories are all so real in later life to your conscious mind and body.

The single biggest cause of dis-ease is your past, emotional baggage, trapped baggage, in fact, 90% of the pain is caused by trapped emotions, the energy that stays with us after an emotional event. Drugs will only suppress them; symptoms are the body crying out there is something wrong here. The imbalances that we suffer from are what ultimately manifest as dis-ease within the mind or body.

> *"People have given their health to their doctor.*
> *Their money to their banker, their soul to the preacher,*
> *their children to the school system,*
> *and in doing so have lost the power to control their lives"*
>
> *'Rolling Thunder'*

Thoughts with feelings strengthen the outcome

If you can change your thoughts and actions, you are going to have a new experience. When you are in the midst of a new experience all of your 5 senses are activated. They are gathering up new information about what you are seeing, smelling, tasting, hearing and feeling, creating a new emotion. The easiest way to get inside of any emotion is through feeling. Always think of what you want (maybe to have a happy healthy body), then feel how you will feel when you have achieved it. Adding feeling and emotion to thought will make it stronger, bring it alive. Thinking of what you don't want is a big mistake, as it will attract it just as fast as thinking what you 'DO WANT'.

If you focus on a headache, it gets worse, then your emotions get involved; you're in chaos and you think you need a drug to kill the pain. The drug may relieve it but will also block the electrical signal in your brain. You need to get to the source, the toxic thought, food or drink that has triggered it that has caused the emotion. You need to cut to the source and clear it. Pain can diminish. (If you feel a headache coming on drink lots of water as you are more than likely dehydrated and rub the tip of your big toes, (reflexology) they will be sore, keep rubbing until the pain goes. Your headache will also go.

I love many of the old sayings and here's another, "If you keep doing what you always did, you will continue to get the same results", whether it be healing and happiness or dis-ease in mind or body, where your attention and energy goes, it grows. Your mind does what it thinks you want, what you keep telling it.

If you allow an emotion to last for hours or days, it is called a **'mood'**. We all know when someone is in a good or bad mood.

If an event happened 5 days ago and you are memorising your emotional reaction, and you keep the same emotional reaction lasting for weeks, months or years, it is called a **'temperament'**. You may ask someone who has an angry temperament, why they are so angry or how they are? Bad mistake, you will hear about it for at least 5 minutes- well ......such 'n such happened to me 6 months ago, poor me and on it goes. Yes, they are living the same emotional reaction.

If we keep those same negative experiences running years on end, it becomes a **'personality trait'**. These people are living in "victim mode", having a lifelong pity party, always asking 'why me.' My answer to that is; It is because you are not listening to the words you are using constantly or taking notice of the movies, the pictures you are creating in your mind. Yes, I am repeating it, 'you create your life by the words you use and the picture you create in your mind'.

So, if you want to change your personality or trait and live in "Victor mode", you need to look at the emotions you have memorised and have stored in your subconscious mind and body. You need to do a check-up from the neck up and take control of your thinking, the words you keep repeating and the pictures you are replaying in your mind.

If you are emotionally upset, get outside and take a walk-in nature, preferably in bare feet, it will ground you, re-establish and clear your energy. **Life is not about what happens to you,** it's all about how you choose to respond to what happens. Start living in the moment and be aware of your thoughts and feelings, what you are saying to yourself and others. You will be surprised at what you have been repeating. You will change your life if you consciously start living in the moment, live in awareness and adjust your course, your words and thoughts accordingly. Surprise yourself. What you focus on will persist. We learn and form habits by repetition. Are you getting the message? ☺

Form good new habits.

*"Always remember the past is history,
The future is a mystery and the present is a gift, enjoy it."*

*"Life is like a deck of cards,
it is how you deal with them that determines the outcome."*

Self-Esteem

What you think about yourself does matter 119
Set up a self-esteem Bank 126
Empowering from within 128
Self-help exercise to improve your self-esteem 132

Ethics of Life
Before you Pray – Believe
Before you Speak – Listen
Before you Spend – Earn
Before you Write – Think
Before you Quit – Try
Before you Die – Live

'Unknown Author'

What you think about yourself does matters

Self-esteem is not an option; it is essential, a necessity for healthy living.

Why do we take what others think and turn it against ourselves? A healthy self-esteem helps you break away from the fear of being humiliated by others.

Your self-image issues are memories trapped in your subconscious mind, no matter what they are- lack of money, over or under weight, I am not enough, whatever memory: they are programming from the past which needs to be addressed.

What YOU think about YOU is what matters. Not what you think others think about you.

The only mind you can change is your own. As long as you act and think positively and your thoughts and actions are aligned with your true values, your truth, who cares what others think. How others think is their business.

So, what is Self-esteem?

It is the general opinion a person has about him or herself, the level to which you respect and value yourself as an important, worthwhile person. It is the level of your mental fitness, how you can handle the ups and downs as they arise in your life.

A low self-esteem is when you feel you are not good enough, insignificant, and unimportant. In reality you are reacting to or recalling what someone has said or done to you in the past and allowing that person to make you feel small, insignificant, and unimportant, with a low self-esteem.

Low self-esteem is being afraid of other people – what they think and how they behave toward you. In reality, that is more indicative of *their* self-esteem.

Having high but realistic self-esteem is essential to good mental and physical health.

A person with a high self-esteem feels terrific about themselves and their life is flowing.

There is also a false self-esteem - Trying to get others approval is insecurity, a low self-esteem. Bragging and showing off, trying to prove one's self, is false self-esteem. Any time you feel better than someone else means that you think that someone is better than you – We are all equal; don't look down on someone else. Judging others is a sign of insecurity, you are trying to make yourself look better.

How much you like and respect yourself also determines the quality of your relationships with other people.

Spending time worrying about things instead of solving them is low self-esteem.

Avoiding conflict with people and not being able to stand up for yourself is low self-esteem.

As I said your self- identity, image and self-esteem are just memories – We talked earlier about everything being stored in your subconscious mind. It is not what happens to you, but how you replay it, what you perceived was said or happened to you. Keep in mind that every time you revisit something that has happened to you, it changes. It's a bit like a Chinese whisper, it changes every time it is said or replayed. Everything that happens is just neutral, there's no good or bad, it just is and you take it in and you make up a story about it. It is a good lesson to learn from.

Everyone perceives things differently. A lot depends on previous conditioning and experiences as to how each person processes an event.

One thing that everyone needs to learn and remember, is that you are never alone, you are always with yourself, so you need to like who you are; like your own company. Your mood is your choice and your mood is catchy, so choose a joyful mood and stay away from grumpy people. The one person you can never get away from is you, so love, respect, believe in and nurture yourself. This is something that took me many years to realise. My self-esteem as a teenager was pretty low. I have always said that I went to school to eat my lunch, I never felt confident or clever, and I felt frumpy, not particularly beautiful. Would you call that low self-esteem? I would.

A teacher once said to me 'why aren't you like your sister?' I felt picked on, I never felt that I was good enough in many ways. If only I knew then that I felt just like more than half of the girls at school, things might have been a little different. Most people don't feel that they are enough, good enough, thin enough, clever enough, strong enough and so on. This thinking usually comes from something someone has said to us, and many carry these thoughts and feelings well into the adulthood.

Many things can knock your self-esteem, especially in your teens and young adult years. But with Google these days, there is so much information and help out there. There are counsellors, many courses and a lot of amazing free information.

However, we also need to be aware of the many social media sites. They can be very detrimental. I had a 16-year-old client with low self-esteem, almost suicidal due to things done and said to her in the past; she felt ugly and fat, she hated herself. She turned to social media and ended up anorexic and bulimic through following models on Instagram, very dangerous.

Texting instead of face-to-face communication, especially when arguing with a friend or partner, is also a ridiculous practice of many couples which causes major issues these days. You cannot hear the tone of voice and meanings often get misinterpreted. This can shoot your self-esteem down real fast. Your imagination runs wild; you create pictures in your mind and start imagining things that aren't true. Once again, the words you say to yourself and the pictures you create in your mind create your life.

No matter whether it was your fault or you perceive it to be someone else's fault that has squashed your self-esteem, you do have the control panel. You have power over your mind if you choose to use it; you need to take responsibility for your life. You are an adult now and can look at it through your adult eyes, not as that young person.

So to identify what or who is causing your disempowerment, your dis-ease, your low self-esteem, you need to look at how you are living, with who you spend most of your time, what you are eating and thinking and start loving yourself and your body. Get help if you don't know where to start.

There are many exercises in this book to help you on your way, but only if you do them!

"To know, and not yet to do, is not yet to Know"

Learn to be happy, don't say you will be happy when you get this or that, it won't work, and you will always be searching. Be grateful for the good and not so good things you have in your life now. Learn from and change the not so good and focus on the good, start believing in yourself and know that you are just like millions of other people.

Start telling yourself good things about yourself every day, and repeat it several times a day, even if you think it is false. When you affirm good things, they will become real. However, you need to make sure that you don't nuke it. If you say for example 'I am a great person' and then follow it in your mind or aloud with 'what a load of crap', you have just cancelled your affirmation and guess what? You are back to where you started. It is ok to lie to yourself if it is for the good. Believe me, it works.

Your subconscious mind is most accessible when you are going to sleep and, in the morning, when you are waking up, because your brainwaves are in the right frequency. So, it makes good sense to do your affirmations at this time, when your brain is in a more receptive state.

If you have negative people in your life, avoid them as much as you can and if you can't get away from them, find help, someone to talk to about it. Be aware, there are people (narcissists) that will try to keep you under their wing. It could be a partner, parent or friend; a narcissist will be so nice one minute and next they are manipulating you with kind words, love and affection. It is mental abuse, which at times is worse than physical abuse, neither are good. These people will drain your energy and control you. Don't let this happen or you will be unhappy most of the time and your self-esteem will be zero.

Your childhood experiences have a great impact on shaping your self-esteem. Your parents, teachers, siblings and friends have all had a powerful impact on how your self-esteem has developed and how you feel about yourself now. With the work I do with many adults, I find that most of their self-esteem issues and dis-ease comes from their childhood. It is as if that young child is still running their lives.

If that is the case with you, you need to go within and talk to that inner child, tell them that you are now looking after them and you are in control, you are now running your life. Tell them that you are no longer that little child. You are a grown adult, that they are within you and safe, you are looking after them and no one can ever hurt them again. You are an adult and need to take charge and responsibility.

Stop blaming others for how you are feeling. Now that you are an adult, you have choices. Either to let go and move on or stay a prisoner of your past life. Speak to yourself, encourage yourself. No one will encourage you more than you. Remember the words you say to yourself and the pictures you create in your mind create your life. Every cell in your body and your subconscious mind hears what you are saying to yourself, and they believe you. Put yourself first, love yourself and you will shine and have energy to give to others. Everyone is unique, you are unique, there is no one else just like you, you are unique in your own right. Just know it and love who you are.

As an adult, you need to have and maintain a healthy self-esteem, to love yourself for who you are, love and maintain your values and what you stand for. If we don't maintain a healthy self-esteem, we are easily knocked off our perch by others; the expectations and opinions of work colleagues, bosses, family, friends and the many types of media we are subjected to,.

Everyone likes and needs to be treated with love, respect, and kindness. Especially children while growing up, to ensure they develop a positive self-esteem. If a child is treated poorly, is overly teased, told they will never amount to anything and made to feel worthless, that child's self-esteem can suffer major long-term damage.

Self-Esteem

Everyone likes to feel loved, important to family and friends and get praise for their achievements. They like to feel important, to feel that they fit in and know that others value their opinions. The higher your self-esteem, the smaller the risk that you will be fixated on what you perceive as your shortcomings.

*"Don't compare your life to others.
There's no comparison between the sun and the moon,
They both shine when it is their time."*

Set up a self-esteem bank

With a bank account, you have to put money in to be able to withdraw. If you withdraw more than you have put in, your account will be over drawn, in the red; you will have an unhealthy bank account, Right? Well your self-esteem bank works the same way, you need to make deposits to boost your self-esteem, fill your bank regularly with praise, love and goodwill to keep it healthy. You cannot draw on what you don't have and stay healthy at the same time. So, keep your self-esteem bank full and healthy. Sometimes we need to praise ourselves, pat ourselves on the back; especially if no one else does.

Many years ago, I was addressing a Probus group of 60 plus elderly ex business men and women. I stood on the stage and asked "how many of you can get up in the morning, look in the mirror and tell the person you see that you love them?" there was silence in the room and interesting looks on faces, many were stunned by the question. I went on to say "I am not being facetious, if you can't love yourself, how can you have love to give to others or expect others to love you." It got some interesting responses. Later, over a cup of tea, I had a few come up to me and say 'well that made me think', especially the men who would never have thought to love themselves, let alone look in the mirror and say it.

A healthy self-esteem is so important for healthy living, so love and believe in yourself. Always remember, others' opinions are just that, their opinion and not necessarily yours, so stick to your guns. The only person you can change is you; the only person others can change is themselves. It is good to ask for and listen to others opinions, but always stay true to your values, believe in and value them.

This is a fun one! Seriously though, focus on laughing more. Laughter will enhance your self-esteem, whether this means reading jokes, watching a funny movie, or just hanging out with friends who always make you laugh. Get more laughter into your life. Stay away from nay-sayers, negative people; they only take you down to their level and deplete your self-esteem bank.

'Life is like riding a horse and the horse is taking you where it wants to go.
You need to take control'

'Caroline Myss'

Empowering from within

I love this story:

A young woman went to her mother grizzling about her life and how things were so hard for her. She did not know how she was going to make it and wanted to give up. She was tired of fighting and struggling. It seemed as one problem was solved, a new one arose.

Her mother took her to the kitchen. She filled three pots with water and placed each on the stove. Soon the pots came to boil. In the first she placed a carrot, in the second she placed an egg, and in the last she placed ground coffee beans. She let them sit and boil; without saying a word.

In about twenty minutes, she turned off the burners. She fished the carrot out and placed it in a bowl. She pulled the egg out and placed it in a bowl. Then she ladled the coffee out and placed it in a bowl. Turning to her daughter, she asked, ' Tell me what you see.'

'Carrot, egg, and coffee,' she replied.

Her mother brought her closer and asked her to feel the carrot. She did and noted that it was soft. The mother then asked the daughter to take the egg and break it. After pulling off the shell, she observed the hardboiled egg.

Finally, the mother asked the daughter to sip the coffee. The daughter smiled as she tasted its rich aroma. The daughter then asked, 'what does it mean, mother?'

Her mother explained that each of these objects had faced the same adversity: boiling water. Each reacted differently. The carrot went in strong, hard, and unrelenting. However, after being subjected to the boiling water, it softened and became weak. The egg had been fragile, its thin outer shell had protected its liquid interior, but after sitting through the boiling water, its inside became hardened. The ground coffee beans were unique, however. After they were in the boiling water, they had changed the water itself.

'Which are you?' she asked her daughter. 'When adversity knocks on your door, how do you respond? Are you a carrot, an egg or a coffee bean?

Wow, she definitely needed a check-up from the neck up. This is a great example of how we manifest our lives by the "words we say and the pictures we create in our mind."

Think of this: Which am I? Am I the carrot that seems strong, but with pain and adversity do I wilt and become soft and lose my strength?

Am I the egg that starts with a malleable heart, but changes with the heat? Did I have a fluid spirit, but after a death, a breakup, a financial hardship or some other trial, have I become hardened and stiff? Does my shell look the same, but on the inside am I bitter and tough with a stiff spirit and hardened heart?

Or am I like the coffee bean? The bean actually changes the hot water, the very circumstance that brings the pain. When the water gets hot, it releases the fragrance and flavour. If you are like the bean, when things are at their worst, you get better and change the situation around you. When the hour is darkest and trials are their greatest, do you elevate yourself to another level? How do you handle adversity? Are you a carrot, an egg or a coffee bean?

May you have enough happiness to make you sweet, enough trials to make you strong, enough sorrow to keep you human and enough hope to make you happy.

The happiest of people don't necessarily have the best of everything; they just make the most of everything that comes their way. The brightest future will always be based on a forgotten past; you can't go forward in life until you let go of your past failures and heartaches. You can't look backwards and get ahead.

When you were born, you were crying and everyone around you was smiling.

Live your life so at the end, you're the one who is smiling and everyone around you is sad that you have gone but may be smiling because they were happy that you were in their life and now flying free.

So, what are you? A carrot, an egg, or a coffee bean? Me, I am the coffee bean with a little milk, but without sugar, as it won't help my body or brain.

I hope that you too are a coffee bean, so everyone around you will be caught by your optimism and smile, because when you are positive you energise and lift yourself and others. Life is a mirror; people will see themselves in you. If you want something to happen, it means that you have to believe in it yourself.

"Perfection is a dis-ease of a nation. We overlay our faces with tons of make-up.
We get Botox and even starve ourselves to become that perfect size.
We try to fix something but you can't fix what you can't see.
It's the soul that needs the surgery. It's time that we take a stand.
How can you expect someone else to love you if you don't love yourself?

You have to be happy with yourself. It doesn't matter what you look like on the outside, it's what's on the inside that counts. I know I have wrinkles on my skin but I want you to see beyond that. I want to embrace the real me and I want you to embrace who you are, the way you are, and love yourself just the way you are."

'Julia Roberts'

Self-help exercise to improve your self-esteem

Get yourself a sheet of paper and answer the questions below to identify your self-esteem and self-image. With your eyes closed, take a few deep breaths and then ask each question. Just sit with the question for a minute or two, the answer will come. Write down what comes to mind first, don't think too hard, just let the answers come; trust yourself, your sense of self, your intuition. Be honest with yourself and do it alone, no one else needs to see your answers. They are for you to know and improve yourself.

- Describe how you see yourself, how you live your life.
- How does the image I hold of myself impact my life?
- How much time do I spend waiting for others' approval?
- How often do I make decisions based on what I think others would think?
- Do I allow myself to be knocked back, humiliated by others?
- Do I allow others to impact on my life? If so how?

This is your HABIT of being, not necessarily who you are. You can change your life and improve your confidence by looking at and working on your strengths rather than your weaknesses.

Ask yourself the following questions and write down the answers.

1. What are my greatest strengths?
2. What lies do I keep telling myself? (i.e., I am a loser, I am fat, I drink too much, I am not lovable, I am not enough etc.)

Now for each of the statements in question 2, ask yourself:

- Are these statements really true?
- If you said yes, ask yourself how do I know it is true?

- Did anyone ever tell me this? or did I make it up myself?
- Ask again, is it really true?
- If so, then how do I know it is true?

You will generally find that it is not true. If it is, then start working towards changing it.

Take all of your strengths and reverse the lies to see the real you.

So, what needs to change to be the real you with a high self-esteem?

Imagining the person you want to be, ask yourself and write down your answers to the following questions.

1. When I change and become the person I want to be, how will I feel?
2. How will I act?
3. What will be possible?

Guess what the primary cause of your results is?

That's right. "YOUR Attitude", the words you say to yourself and the pictures you create in your mind. *"If it is to be, it is up to me "*

Most people try to fix themselves from the outside, (from other people, possessions, diets etc).

Everything you need is within you.

It is important to tell yourself the truth. Believe in yourself and trust your intuition.

The following is an exercise to help you identify your downfalls, to learn what you need to work with in the future to build and strengthen your self-esteem, your self-worth.

Read each statement and rate yourself, your beliefs, honestly from 0-10 (10 being Yes)

1. I feel that I am good enough.
2. I have phenomenal coping skills.
3. I love myself.
4. I am intelligent.
5. I easily say "No" when asked to do something I don't want to do.
6. I do not feel guilty when I stand up for myself.
7. Money comes to me when I need it, I have enough.
8. People enjoy being with me.
9. I am in control of my power.
10. I enjoy spending time with others.
11. I am an interesting person.
12. I have a great memory.
13. I have unique talents and skills.
14. I have positive close relationships with people in my life.
15. I do not take others actions or words personally.
16. I deserve good things in life.
17. I forgive myself easily when I make mistakes.
18. I forgive myself and let go of past mistakes.
19. I forgive others for their mistakes.
20. I am proud of my accomplishments to date.
21. I am not afraid to try new things.
22. I keep my commitments.

23. I spend more time solving my problems instead of worrying about them.
24. I address conflict directly instead of hiding or wishing they would go away.
25. I am a good communicator.

Don't beat yourself up if you have a low score, just start working on the low ones and retake the test to see how you are improving in these areas every few weeks.

Doing this work will change your subconscious core beliefs. It will help reprogram your mind. When you become aware and start recognising the ANT's in your life and IF and only if you take action, it will change your self-beliefs, your self-esteem and turn your life around.

To build your self-esteem create affirmations from the list of statements above, especially the ones you scored low on, from the previous section on forgiveness and letting go, or create new ones that resonate with you.

Here's a great tool to use if you are constantly angry or sad: Put a rubber band on your wrist and every time you think a negative thought about yourself, curse or swear stretch it and let it go. Ouch. This will help you to become aware of your thoughts so you can make changes.

As I mentioned earlier only angry, unhappy people swear (Unless of course it has just become a habit from when they were angry) so start working on yourself to find out what is making you unhappy or angry, take action to rectify it.

Life is amazing when you are happy and in control.

Keep your commitments to yourself and others, and don't make promises you can't keep, set achievable goals, and celebrate when you achieve them.

When you have a problem, think of the solutions or possibilities instead of focusing on the problem and worrying about it. Be positive and say "What if I could........" or "What if I did........" and feel how you feel about the outcome. When you put feelings with saying, writing or imagining goals they will be much stronger. When you achieve a goal, you boost your self-esteem, so celebrate.

Connect with your inner self for answers, through feeling it in your heart space and/ or your solar plexus and activate your imagination.

Learn to say "NO" without feeling guilty.

Surround yourself with supportive, positive people who are confident and fill your Self-esteem bank.

Be aware of those ANT's in your mind and recognise that inner critic. Did you know that you are harder on yourself than anyone else ever is; you are your biggest critic so start praising yourself. ☺ Give yourself self-approval rather than relying on the approval of others.

Learn to take criticism as either constructive or someone else's negative projection that has nothing to do with you, just let it go over your head.

Words are energy and can lift you or cut you down – When you shift the 's' in the word 'WORDS' you create a 'SWORD'. So be aware of the word you use and those you accept from others.

Come up with reasonable goals and standards of behaviour for yourself. (Avoid impossible goals and perfection). Step outside of your comfort zone with confidence. Know you can do it, believe in yourself. Self-confidence brings positive changes in your life.

If you continue to feed your mind with things that do not serve you, your life, self-esteem and values become depleted. So, don't worry, be happy ☺ Keep smiling.

"Your mind is like a garden; keep out the weeds,
Plant and nurture the flowers and fruits that will nourish you"

"I love the ones who stay in my life and make me happier.
I also love the ones who left my life and made me stronger"

Control Your Stress - Change Your Life

What is Stress? **139**
Reduce Stress – Declutter **144**
Laughter can cure **147**
Take Control of your Thoughts **149**

"Don't believe everything you think. Thoughts are just
that–thoughts."
'Alan Lokos'

"Our Words reveal our Thoughts,
Our Manners mirror our Self-esteem,
Our Actions reflect our Character
Our Habits predict our Future."

What is stress?

So, what is stress and what can it do to you?

This is a big question, as many variances can trigger it and it can affect people in many different ways.

Stress can start from things as small as worrying about what others will think, to the 'what ifs', what if I ......? what if they....?, to peer pressure, work pressure, deadlines, relationships, business success or not, verbal or physical abuse, to I am not enough – good enough, strong enough, loveable enough, clever enough, thin enough, whatever enough. Goodness that looks like everyone and everything in life. Yes, we need to love ourselves, believe in ourselves, know that we are enough as we are and to learn not to stress about things.

The definition of Stress varies from dictionary to dictionary, however the most common is "a feeling of strain and pressure".

SO DON'T SWEAT THE SMALL STUFF.

Nothing is big or small, good or bad, young or old, not good enough unless you compare it against something else. Everything just is what it is, and if it is something you can't change, why allow it to upset you. If it is something you can change, take action and do something about it.

If you hold onto a glass of water for 5 minutes, it will not be heavy; however, if you hold onto the same glass for hours, it will feel heavier and heavier. Just like any worries, problem and resentment, past events that you are stressing yourself over. Sort it or drop it, let go.

'Let go' are two of the biggest little words there are. When you let go you relieve yourself of pressure, stress, and pain, the longer you hold on the worse it will get. Just like the old saying 'We too, often turn molehills into mountains. As mentioned many times, you create your life by the words you say and the pictures we create in your mind.

You have probably heard the story of Aladdin where he found a magic lamp with a Genie inside? He just rubbed it, asked a question and the Genie delivered. When you say "I am", the words that follow are summoning **creation with a mighty force,** because you are declaring it to be fact, stating it with certainty.

Immediately after you say, "I am tired" or "I am broke" or "I am sick" or "I am late" or "I am overweight" or "I am old".....the Genie, your subconscious mind, says, "Your wish is my command." Words have a magical power within.

Here are a few questions to ponder. Be honest....

1. Are you creating your stress?
2. Do you keep saying my life sucks?
3. Are you unhappy with your body?
4. Are you unhappy with your weight?
5. Are you unhappy with your partner?
6. Do you keep saying I don't have enough money to make ends meet?
7. Do you lack that special someone in your life and think you can't attract them?
8. Does your life suck? If you say so it will.

I think of stress as pressure that causes dis-ease of the body and mind. Stress is the main cause of most, if not all, dis-ease in your life. It causes many problems physically, emotionally and mentally from small annoyances, heart and mental problems to cancer. Too much stress will inhibit your immune system.

Take note of what is causing your stress, causing discomfort or pain; be aware of your thoughts and actions. Stress can be avoided if caught early enough. If you do a check-up from the neck up when you are starting to stress out, to identify the irritations in your life, be aware of what you are saying, telling yourself, you can then take action and remedy it. Try living in the present rather than in the past or future. This will allow you to take better control of your life.

Oops, I just used a word I tell my clients to remove from their vocabulary. "Try". When you try something, there is leaving room for not succeeding; it has an element of failure in it! Just do it.

I was recently stressed and contracted a urinary tract infection, I hadn't had one for 30-plus years, my stomach also became irritated and then I ended up with a cold, I literally felt like a weak rag doll. 'Wow,' I thought to myself. 'What on earth is happening here?' So I went within. I did a check-up from the neck up (I got out of my head and went within to ask myself what my thinking was that was causing my stress and dis-ease within my body).

I found I had been allowing myself to be irritated by other people that I had been spending time with, including myself. Yes, I was also irritated with myself for judging others and not handling the situation I was in.

Most stress and dis-ease come from within, from our thinking. When you change your thinking and perception of an event and situation you can stop stressing yourself and turn your health and life around.

There are different kinds of stress.

People experience and respond to stress in different ways.

- ➢ Some have an angry or agitated stress response - They're heated, keyed up, overly emotional, and unable to sit still,

they lash out at whatever or whoever is unfortunate to be close.
- ➢ Some just moan about how much they have to do and how lousy they feel – this hurts, that hurts.
- ➢ Others have a withdrawn or depressed stress response. They shut down, space out, and show very little energy or emotion, they go quiet and within themselves, not knowing how to handle it.
- ➢ Some become tense and frozen. They "freeze" under pressure and can't do anything. They look paralysed, but under the surface, they are extremely agitated.
- ➢ Others hold it in their body and it manifests as a dis-ease – Organ, skin, back pain, tumours, depression, etc.

This shows that the management of stress is different for everyone.

Stress can kill, believe me, I have seen it many times; people just can't accept that stress is causing their illness, especially the No # 1 stress killer, 'cancer.' Nine times out of ten it has come from their thinking and how they respond or react to a situation. And, they don't or won't recognise or accept that it is stress.

I recommend you check out EFT (Emotional Freedom Technique). This is tapping on meridian points sending calming signals to the 'Amygdala' which is a section of the brain that is responsible for detecting fear and preparing for emergency events, it is your fight or flight response centre that activates when you are stressed.

Tapping rewires your body and brain to make better decisions, to take back control, and take better actions. It changes your energy and you feel better, with more confidence, helping you to release trauma, emotions, and pain.

Stress causes depression. The more sugar you have the more hell you will create in your body. Getting rid of added sugar in your diet will help you control depression (Eat fruit to get your sugar fix). Plus, cancer thrives on sugar.

Free Antidepressants that are more effective than drugs

- 30 minutes sunshine a day is the most important effective antidepressant.
- 30 minutes of exercise is the next most important effective antidepressant.
- Laughter, smiles and hugs.
- Sit and walk with your back straight, head up, chin pulled in a little, shoulders up and back. Oh, and put a smile on your face. Now feel how you feel.
- Drink plenty of good clean toxin-free water and get plenty of fresh air to flush out the toxins.

You can simply be alive for 90 years or you can live 90 years, you have a choice.

I choose to live my 90 plus years.

"You can rise up from anything.
You can completely recreate yourself.
You are not stuck you have choices.
You can think new thoughts you can learn new things.
You can create new habits.
The main thing is that you start today and never look back"

Reduce Stress - declutter

One of the best ways to make you feel good about yourself and reduce stress in your life is by decluttering your mind and life. It will relieve stress leading you to a happier healthier life. Most of us have a mind full of clutter. Mental clutter is a lot worse than having a cluttered home or workspace, in saying that however, a cluttered environment adds to a cluttered mind and vice versa. If your environment is cluttered it will send you into confusion. A cluttered mind is restless and unfocused. It tries to move in many different directions at once and the result is, very little gets done; you go around in circles creating stress. Can you relate to that?

So, let's look at what you might need to declutter in your life.

Firstly, your mind – A cluttered mind could include any or all of the following: worrying about the future; reliving the past, holding onto past events; keeping a mental to-do list; complaints; trying to juggle work and family, to name a few.

Harmony on the inside correlates with harmony on the outside. One good thing about having a well-organised, uncluttered space is that it helps calm your mind. If you are in a living or working environment that is chaotic and cluttered constantly, you will start to feel chaotic on the inside. However, even if your "outside" environment is reasonably organised there are still times when you need to work on, decluttering your mind, the "inside".

Other possible stressors affecting your life could be the people you spend most of your time with, your family and friends who could be draining your energy, filling your mind with 'what if's' - Do I have to do ...?- Do I have to check...? – Too many emails – phone calls, spending too much unproductive time on the internet and/or with people that are not adding to your life.

Many years ago, I heard a saying which I love, "get rid of the people in your mind that are bugging you and not paying rent".

So, identify what or who is cluttering your mind and start fixing it!

Secondly- Is your car clean and tidy, your garage, house- bedroom, kitchen, wardrobe, your workspace / desk organised, just to name a few. Wow, the list is exhausting. But think about it, if you are so overloaded with options, feeling guilty, too many things to do or think about, can't find things, have unhealthy relationships, the stress just grows and turns into dis-ease one way or another.

Fortunately, there are things you can do to clean out some space in your head, to declutter and destress. Below are a few suggestions to help declutter and gain more clarity, less overwhelm and get more done, it will also ease your stress levels.

Use a diary; if you haven't got one, then I suggest you get one with an area for notes. When you think of something you need to do or discuss with someone, write it down and once a week, prioritise what you need to do. If you need to diarise an appointment, do so rather than trying to remember and cluttering your mind. Check your diary daily.

Be careful of what you are *letting into your mind*, taking onboard, your subconscious mind will file it. Live consciously; be aware of what is happening in your mind and life constantly. Limit your time on the internet, emails, texts. Also be mindful of what you are reading and listening to – Newspapers, magazines, blogs, social media posts and watching on TV. Limit the bad news and rubbish that is bombarding your brain constantly through the radio and TV and negative posts on social media. Unsubscribe to irrelevant posts, emails, blogs, etc. Only read material that contributes to your wellbeing or is relaxing or exciting. Decide what is relative and discard the rest. Emails are major clutter. If your inbox is full of mail you haven't made decisions on. You will become more and more frustrated and keep thinking you haven't got time to go through them. You will be worried about deleting them all as you might delete something you needed. Stop! Find time to go through them and delete, once you are on top of them stay on top of them. Prioritise your days and set aside 10 – 15 mins to check and action emails. You will feel so much better.

Physical clutter messes with your head – If your car, house, garden or workplace are cluttered, untidy, messy, your mind will also be. You will always be thinking there is something to do, something to clean up, looking for something you know you put in a safe place (but where), which can be mentally exhausting and a waste of time, a major stressor. So, declutter your living and work environments and you will declutter your mind.

Don't try to do it all at once. Write a list, prioritise the tasks and set goals, (make sure that your goals are doable, keep them small). You can only do one thing at a time properly so no multi-tasking, are you listening ladies? I had to laugh when I wrote this as I am a big multi-tasker. Prioritise, do one job/declutter at a time and complete it. Start with one thing, stay focused on it until it is completed and forget everything else for that time. Turn your phone off and stop thinking of other things you could be doing, put your heart into the task in hand. If you start to veer off to something else, or your mind keeps wandering, bring it back to the task in hand. Be aware and focused and you will breeze through it, you will feel so proud of yourself when you start checking things off your list. Reward yourself when you have achieved each little goal. Take time for yourself, relax.

Say to yourself daily "I turn every experience into an opportunity".
"Before God, we are all equally wise – and equally foolish"

Albert Einstein

Laughter can cure

We have just looked at many things you can change to declutter your mind and body, but there are so many other factors that can change your stress levels and life.

Stress really does do a number on your mental health and body; laughter is a great way to kill stress.

Make it your mission to have a good deep belly laugh every day; it will do wonders for your mood and wellbeing. See if there is a laughter yoga club in your district if so, join it. Or go onto YouTube and look up 'Try not to laugh'.

Laughter and smiles play a big part in healing. Life can run a smoother path when we indulge in generous amounts of laughter and smiles. Laugh for no reason.

Charlie Chaplin wrote; **"Laughter is the tonic, the relief, the surcease from pain".** Yes, laughter is certainly a tonic, it is an extension of joyful positive emotions, it is an expression of pleasure, which gives a renewed vigour for life. Laughter calms, relaxes and deeply de-stresses. Smiles go a long way too. ☺

A sense of humour and a really good laugh are more healing to the body and mind than any medication will ever be. When you laugh your perception shifts, you release feelings of judgment, blame and self-pity, bringing a better understanding of yourself and others. It brings a response from the universe with an uplifting feeling.

Smiles and laughter are 'giving' activities when you share them you are giving and receiving.

It increases your sense of wellbeing and gives meaning and purpose to life.

A common cause of deep stress is the belief that you have no use in life. Giving may correct this imbalance for you.

We are all healers and laughter is considered the best medicine by many. We can if we choose, positively affect others with loving, unconditional energy simply by sharing a smile or laughter. Passing on a smile, or sharing laughter is merely giving love and warmth to that person and yourself.

Laughter and smiles have a deep effect on your bodies systems. Laughter gets more oxygen into your lungs, deepening respiration, it increases circulation, speeds tissue healing, improves your stamina and concentration, it stimulates the body's hormonal system, releasing your happy hormones, it increases white blood cells, and generally supports every system in your body. And of course, it is free to give and receive.

Laughter is a great anti-ager and anti-anger – So why would you not want to do it?

As the saying goes – "When you smile the whole world smiles with you".

A Smile didn't come out of thin air.
Someone had to create atmosphere
"Let your SMILE change the world,
But don't let the world change your SMILE."

'Unknown Author'

Take control of your thoughts

To live a happy, healthy, stress-free life, you need to take control of YOUR MIND, your Automatic Negative Thoughts. YOUR mind is the only mind you have control of and if you don't take control of it, it will control you. Your thoughts are so very powerful; they will control your life if you let them. Your mind can run away on you if you don't take control of it. When you take control of your mind you take control of your life.

Many get stressed by allowing others behaviours and opinions affect them, someone else's opinion doesn't have to be your reality. Or they get upset because they can't change someone else. Too many try to change other people, they do not realise that they cannot control anybody else let alone their mind. You can't change another person; they have to change themselves. So, if you are getting stressed and frustrated, trying to change others, in particular, your partner or friends, quit trying now because they won't change unless they feel or realise that they need to and have to do it themselves. They may even be happy with who they are. You could consider trying to influence them by leading by example and hoping they will change, but don't stress yourself, it is not worth it. Relationships are major stressors if there is a lack of communication and balance.

The main causes of stress are our everyday life activities which can be full of hassles, deadlines, frustrations, technology, finances and demands from relationships with the boss, parents, partners, children, peers or yourself. For many people, stress is so commonplace that it has become a way of life. We need to learn not to sweat the small stuff.

'No one can upset you unless you give them permission' - Eleanor Roosevelt.

Another awakening for some is learning that not everything that you think is true, and your thoughts can be very damaging to your body.

Here's something to get your head around –

'Your mind will affect your body far more than your body will affect your mind'.

You get irritated, you get itchy or a rash will appear because of something you have thought about, said, seen, heard or done. You don't get an irritation without first a thought. It may not be consciously. These thoughts could come from deep in your subconscious mind, triggered by past events.

I have encountered several clients with hearing problems and when asked how long they had had their hearing problem, many replied that they had issues with their ears from a young age. There is a common theme, showing that they came from an unhealthy family environment, their parents argued all of the time or yelled at each other or the kids constantly. So, they tried from an early age to block it out. It is real, some even used to hide under their bed or in the closet to get away from it. Wow, isn't life interesting. How sad is that, their family environment has affected their whole life!!!

So, if you are having hearing problems, there is probably something or someone in your life now or from the past, that you do not want to hear. Or maybe someone at home or work that you can't get away from, you don't want to, but have to listen to.

If you have eye problems, there's probably something in your life you are not wanting to see. Hip problems are all about moving forward in life, worrying about the future, your hips and legs carry you forward in life, people with knee issues are usually stubborn. These are only a few examples; everything starts with a thought. You may not even realise you are having these thoughts or acting in a certain way if you are not living in an awareness, being constantly aware of what is going on in your mind. Excess stress WILL manifest as some type of dis-ease if not recognised and dealt with; it needs to be released somehow.

If you don't change your thinking early enough, the problem becomes bigger and bigger, until there is a point of no return. Such as trying to block hearing something continuously will eventually cause deafness, a sore hip will end up having to be replaced and so on. I have been there and done that; luckily, I caught my thoughts and turned my dis-ease around. So, think how you are thinking, listen to your body, and be aware of arising symptoms, what your body is telling you. You can heal yourself; you can control stress.

Stress isn't always bad. In small doses, it can help you perform under pressure and motivate you to do your best. But when you're constantly running in overload or emergency mode, your mind and body will pay the price.

You can protect yourself by recognizing the signs and symptoms of stress and taking steps to reduce its harmful effects. It's important to learn how to recognize when your stress levels are out of control. Stress can creep up on you. As I said earlier, do a check-up from the neck up regularly, be aware of your thoughts and feelings. And don't allow other people to upset you. Stop stressing your mind and body.

There is no stress or tension in the world. If I give you a shopping bag to go and buy some you won't be able to find any. It is just the way someone is feeling.

"There cannot be a crisis next week.
My schedule is already full"

'Henry Kissinger'

Food – Good or Bad?

Food is energy 153
Are you eating intelligently? 157
We have worldwide epidemics 161
Sugar – How bad and why 162
My take on Fats and Oils 167

"Do the right thing. It will gratify some people and astonish the rest."

Mark Twain

Food is energy

Food will contribute to the creation of a healthy or unhealthy mind and body. You would have heard the saying; "You are what you eat". This is so true.

If you are off-colour, so to speak, the main thing is to identify what is stressing you; is it the food you are eating? If so, start taking action to rectify it, change or eliminate it from your life. Nine times out of ten, the cause of dis-ease is either what you have put in your mouth or mind, or what comes out of them, the food going in, thoughts you are thinking and the words you say.

Adopt a healthy lifestyle; if your life, your mind and body are not balanced you are easily toppled, so make sure you **eat good healthy** food.

Your relationship to your body is important so you need to take good care of yourself, eat and exercise intelligently and think good thoughts.

Most of us know what we need to do; it is just a matter of doing it.

Everything is energy; food, thoughts, and words are all energy and so important to healthy living.

Eating junk food, processed foods, fast foods, sugary foods and drinks, using artificial sweeteners, drinking too much caffeine and alcohol, using hydrogenated vegetable oils and oxidized polyunsaturated fats all add to damaging your health. Whew, that was a mouthful. Each one of these may energise you for a while, when you consume them, you may think they are relieving stress and comforting you. That may be so for a short time, however, eaten or drunk regularly, they can be very toxic and detrimental to your health, adding even more stress to your mind and body and leading to more long term dis-ease.

You can access a lot of information online and in your community from natural health specialists, doctors, herbalists and alternative healers on food, vitamins and minerals and their impact on your health. However, there are conflicting reports; it depends on who has commissioned the research and where the researchers are coming from, their beliefs or what their agenda is.

As said previously, I am no specialist but have read and studied many subjects on healthy living and want to share my thoughts and experiences with you, I could go on forever about the subject, however, I have decided to leave that to the experts and just give a few suggestions; information on things I consider important.

Nurture yourself and go back to nature. Get your healing ingredients and goodness such as Beta carotene, vitamins, and minerals from fruits and vegetables – According to 'Whole Foods Guru', Don Tolman, 'an extensive Harvard study showed that by eating one carrot a day reduced the risk of having a stroke by 68%'. He goes on to say 'you can prevent, relieve, reverse and in many cases cure almost any condition from anaemia to yeast infections by using nothing more than Mother Nature's best medicine – Whole foods and healthy living'.

Another person I recommend taking note of is Medical Medium, "Anthony William". Here is an example of his work:

"Celery juice's undiscovered subgroups of sodium that I call cluster salts protect the liver's cell membranes and inhibit the growth of viruses, bacteria, and fungus. Celery restores the liver's bile production capability as well as the potency and complicated structure of the bile, which in most people is completely imbalanced. Its cluster salts bind onto free-floating poisons and toxins inside the liver and flush them into the bloodstream, remaining bonded so that the troublemakers leave the kidneys or intestinal tract safely.

Celery juice purges the liver while bringing down liver heat to a safe level. It's the ultimate gallbladder rehabilitator, helping to dissolve gallstones over time, making them small enough either not to cause harm or to be able to pass through the bile duct. Celery's sodium also expands the bile duct so it's not restricted, in case a large stone does breach.

Celery juice removes mucus out of the intestinal tract and liver and increases the production of the undiscovered seven-acid blend of hydrochloric acid in the stomach. It also disperses fat cells inside the liver."

Anthony has some good reading in his books, *"Medical Medium" and "Medical Medium Liver Rescue":* He has answers to many dis-eases including Chronic Fatigue Syndrome, MS, Fibromyalgia, Shingles, Eczema, Psoriasis, Diabetes, Strep, Acne, Gout, Bloating, Gallstones, Adrenal Stress, Fatigue, Fatty Liver, Weight Issues, SIBO & Autoimmune Dis-ease. It is worth taking the time to check his work out. I find his books very interesting and informative.

Daniel Amen and many other brain experts are also worth following. Reading their books and listening to them, they stress that what you eat and drink affects your brain. We need to remember that our brain tells our body what to do, so it is worth looking after.

Many spices and herbs are flavour of the day, and there is a good reason for that; they are so good for your health.

Turmeric is one of my favourites; I use it in nearly every meal, including my healthy morning whiz up. It is well known for its healing abilities. This ancient spice has been used as an active ingredient in many Asian dishes, especially in India, for thousands of years. Turmeric has an amazing ability to naturally support your immune system, allowing pain sufferers to finally experience relief and enjoy life again.

Inflammation is just your body's natural response to things like injury, toxins, and infections. When you get sick or injured, your immune system is called in for support, white blood cells rush to the scene. As more and more white blood cells show up, the area becomes tender, warm and swollen. That's why it's called "inflammation." Turmeric helps your immune system to do its job, destroying dangerous invaders and keeping you healthy. When your immune system cannot work effectively it can affect your mood, stress, energy, and metabolism.

Turmeric is part of the ginger family; **Ginger** is another anti-inflammatory. Turmeric also contains **Curcumin**, another amazing healer that improves your cell's response to sugar, according to recent research it slows down the uptake of sugar into the bloodstream

According to Marc S Micozzi, M.D., Ph.D., in his book "The Micozzi Files," a book addressing the cause and natural treatments for cancer and 55 other covered-up cures. He also says "Fewer people progress to Type1 diabetes with curcumin." Micozzi's book uncovers many myths about foods,

Garlic, Sea or Himalayan salts, Pepper, Cinnamon, Pumpkin seeds, Sunflower seeds, Chai seeds, Nuts, Parsley, Sage and the many herbs you can grow in your home garden all have their healing benefits. Who needs a pharmacy? Prevent dis-ease and ill health by eating from nature. There is an abundance of leafy greens, beets, and carrots with their beta-carotene, fruits, berries, and vegetables with their many minerals and vitamins. Food is energy.

"The most powerful pharmacy in the world is between your ears"

Are you eating intelligently?

Could the first step to changing your life be as simple as what you put in your mouth?

From my experience with food and the study I have undertaken, my recommendation is to eat from nature and you can't go wrong.

With so many opinions in the market place and so much advice offered, you need to take note of who is giving you the advice. Is the advice factual, well researched and who did the research? Was it someone with a bias, touting for business, pushing their produce, a scientist, a doctor?

Your body will usually tell you if something is good for you or not, it will reject toxic foods, make you ill or cause some type of discomfort or dis-ease. I often muscle test foods, drinks, vitamins, and minerals to see if they are good for me or not. We talk about muscle testing later.

How you think about the food you eat also has a big impact on how your body reacts to it, how it treats you. If you feel like a treat every now and then, even though you know it is loaded with sugar or whatever, enjoy it, and don't beat yourself up. Just know that it is a once-in-a-while thing and your body will handle it. I really enjoy a nice cream or a great New Zealand pie every now and then.

I am certainly no expert in the field, but research (when needed) and common sense usually prevails with me. Foods grown in the earth ground us, processed foods disempower us. Stay away from processed and fast foods or at best, limit consumption. Get your sugar fix from nature - fruits, and vegetables. Enjoy your food, only eat when you are hungry, eating slowly will also help to avoid indigestion by allowing your metabolism to do its job. Another little hint is to never cook or eat when you are angry or upset; you and others that eat the food are very likely to get indigestion. It is a good idea to clear food before you ingest it. Remove any toxic based energy that may be held in it. Give thanks to everyone that has played a roll in the creation of it, from the grower of the food to your plate. Give gratitude for every meal you consume.

Drink water ½ an hour before and/or ½ an hour after your meal, not with your meal, as it will dilute your digestive juices, slowing down your metabolism.

Your stomach is only the size of your fist, so don't overload and stretch it. You are better to have small meals regularly than overeating. A large meal at night, too close to bedtime, is not good for your metabolism or sleep. Your body has to process the food through the night, and if it is busy trying to process excess food, it is not resting and healing while you sleep.

Have you ever filled your plate at a smorgasbord with way too much, got halfway through it and told yourself…"I'm stuffed, I can't eat anymore.", but then you continue to plough through the rest until your plate is empty, saying to yourself' I have paid for this so I will eat it?' That sounds like my mother; she would never leave anything on her plate, especially if she paid for it at a restaurant.

Even though your stomach is full and maybe starting to hurt, you still keep cramming more and more into your mouth. Guess what? Food is garbage, whether you stuff it in your mouth when your body cannot deal with it or you throw it in the pig bin. Do you think your body was designed to work like that? No, of course not!

The same goes for stuffing yourself with a packet of potato crisps. They are made to make you want more. Junk foods like crisps are filled with so many cocaine-like excitotoxins that your brain is having a dopamine-fuelled firework show, and all you can think about is the next fix, that next bite. I know, I love crisps too, so I never buy them and now and then I have a binge at a party and don't ever beat myself up for it. I rarely do it these days.

Excitotoxins are chemicals either added to food, or found in food that cause an overstimulation of the nervous system, which can cause the cells to be destroyed. These chemicals are found in almost all processed foods. The most common excitotoxins are aspartame (an artificial sweetener) and monosodium glutamate (commonly known as MSG), when consumed, your body goes into overdrive, packing more and more bad fat into every area of your body. Yeeks!!

There are so many varying and controversial opinions on different foods, herbs, meats, gluten-free, sugar, oils and fats, wheat, vitamin and minerals, the list goes on. I have my opinions on many of these, however, as you know, I do not profess to be an expert, so I have only gone more deeply into what has been beneficial for or concerned me.

As for the many differing diets – high fat, low fat, fat-free, vegan, grapefruit, eat for your blood type, keytone, paleo, fasting, on it goes. You could be on a real roller coaster, as most diets work for a little while. You think 'great, I'm fine now. I've lost 10kgs. I can stop the diet and just watch what I eat', or you come to a standstill and stop losing weight. Then, when you go off the diet, you start putting the weight back on, maybe slowly, but usually surely.

There could be any of many reasons why you keep holding onto that weight, including not doing all of the other things that go with building a healthy body, such as exercise and healthy thinking, or subconsciously wanting to cover yourself up to protect yourself.

You need to seek the reason your body is holding onto the weight. If you don't get to the cause of why you keep gaining weight, it will keep coming back. So, what is happening in your subconscious mind? What are you holding onto; pain or resentment? Trying to hide? Why? The cause often stems from something stored in your subconscious mind from an event that happened years ago. It psychologically causes you to comfort-eat and often sabotages your attempt to decrease your weight. So, it doesn't matter how much money and time you spend studying and trying different diets, or what foods you eat. If you don't treat the cause, guess what? Yes, you will struggle to reduce weight and keep it off. So dieting isn't always the answer.

I am so good at changing the subject when I get on my bandwagon. Let's get back to food.

Grow a garden and fruit trees, there is nothing better than picking fresh food that you have grown, and then you know it is fresh and chemical-free. It is also grounding and therapeutic to work with the earth. Let alone the exercise you are going to get preparing it and the money you will save when you can go pick it from your garden.

To live a healthy life, eating intelligently is one component. Living a healthy life is to have balance in mind and body.

"To eat is a necessity, but to eat intelligently is an art."

'François de la Rochefoucauld'

We have worldwide epidemics

Plaguing the world are epidemics of Obesity, Alzheimer's, Type 2 Diabetes, Depression, Anxiety, Cancer and Heart dis-ease. These are all affected by stressing the mind and body one way or another. Your diet is no exception, remember, you are what you eat; excess sugar intake and using the wrong fats and oils are big contributors so I am going to spend a little time talking about sugar, fats, and oils as they have a big impact on so many lives and there is conflicting information out there.

I talked about fast foods, processed foods, and other foods and drinks previously and will most probably do so again, as I want to get the message across loud and clear. They are all toxic to your body if eaten or drunk frequently. I call sugar 'Sweet Poison', it slowly but surely will detrimentally affect your brain and organs. Sugar is a major factor in the cause of Alzheimer's; recently Alzheimer's has been identified as Type 3 Diabetes. It is a hot subject for me because I recently lost my mother twice; firstly, to Alzheimer's and secondly to the heavens above. Sugar is not the only factor that causes these dis-eases but it plays a big part in contributing. I will go into other concerns later, meanwhile back to sugar because I believe it is one of the main causes of our worldwide epidemics.

"Nurturing yourself is loving yourself.
When you love yourself, you will have love to share with others"

Sugar - How bad and why?

The truth is you can't just "burn off" sugar, it's not so simple.

Most people think that if they eat sugar, they can just exercise a little bit harder and they will "burn it off" Unfortunately, that is not so.

We all know that sugar is bad for us, but most people don't truly understand how bad or why it's so bad!

If you knew exactly why sugar is so bad for you and what it does to the cells in your body, I promise that you would think twice about eating that piece of cake, sweets, sugary soft drinks, ice blocks or ice cream, or even worse, feed them to your children.

If that doesn't scare you a little, here are just a few of the reasons that sugar could make you seriously ill, and you know the consequences of that.

Of course, you already know that sugar makes you fat, and gives you excess calories without any beneficial nutrients whatsoever.

- Sugar causes extreme fluctuations in your blood sugar, and excess blood sugar accelerates the rate of aging of your organs, skin, arteries, and joints.
- Sugar also raises your triglycerides to dangerous levels, which can lead you to heart dis-ease. Triglycerides are a type of fat found in your blood. After you eat, your body converts the calories that you don't need into triglycerides and stores them in your fat cells to be used for energy later.
- It causes you to wear out your pancreas and insulin, causing type 2 diabetes.
- Sugar feeds cancer.

- ➤ It also slows down your white blood cells, making an infection more likely, and even allowing cancer cells a better chance to form in your body.
- ➤ It causes tooth decay

I have read so many articles on sugar consumption from NZ to the US and seen many similarities in its effect on our health.

Added sugar is the single worst ingredient in the modern diet. It provides calories with no added nutrients and can damage your metabolism in the long run. Eating too much sugar is linked to weight gain and various dis-eases as mentioned above. Most of these conditions lead to depression and anxiety.

Sugar is hidden in so many foods under many different names; it has crept into nearly every type of processed and fast foods.

A few names you might find it under on a label are:

Glucose, sucrose, maltose, honey, lactose, maple syrup, sugar, dextrose, fructose, fruit juice, corn syrup, barley malt, sorbitol, just to name a few.

The problem is, many foods we buy over the counter, in particular from a bakery, do not have labels.

It is very important to make the distinction between added sugars and sugars that occur naturally in foods like fruits and vegetables. These are healthy foods that contain water, fibre, and various micronutrients. Natural sugars are good, but the same does not apply to added sugar. Added sugar, that is ordinary white refined sugar (sucrose), is the main ingredient in sweets and is abundant in many processed foods like soft drinks, and baked products. Including the New Zealand and Australian-renowned Pavlova. Sorry.

According to the American Heart Association (AHA), the maximum amount of added sugars you should eat in a day are - Men: 150 calories per day (37.5 grams or 9 teaspoons) Women: 100 calories per day (25 grams or 6 teaspoons)- Jun 28, 2018

The NZ Nutrition Foundation in a white paper produced in 2014 suggested - In line with WHO (World Health Organisation) recommendations, NZNF supports the message that less than 10% of energy in the diet should be from 'free sugars'(i.e. sugar added opposed to natural sugar) in an adult with a healthy BMI this equates to a maximum of 50g of sugar per day or 12 teaspoons (Figures show that NZ adult men currently consume 120g of total sugar i.e. intrinsic plus free sugars, per day and adult women 96g)

Interestingly in a US report, over two hundred years ago (1815) the average person consumed about 6.8kg's sugar per year, that is 18gms per day, by 1900 in the US consumption had increased to 38.5kgs per annum, 105.4gms per day and early 2000's consumption was up to 72.6kg's per year, 240gms per day. It is kind of mind-boggling don't you agree?

According to Bruce Fife, in his book 'Stop Alzheimer's now', the average person needs a total intake of 300 grams of carbohydrates per day, given some of those carbohydrates are from the natural sugars in fruit and vegetables. These stats say that over 2/3rds of the 300gms required per day is pure sugar, with no nutritional value or fibre, just calories draining nutrients from the body without replacing them, causing metabolic shock and poor health.

As you can see, there are many different statistics out there, but the message is the same. Cut added sugar out of your diet; your body doesn't need it. Keep in mind that added sugar recommendations are not just the teaspoon or two that you put in your tea or coffee; it is the sugar in the bread, cakes, processed foods, etc. as well.

So, to clarify, when we talk about how much damage sugar does to your body, we're NOT talking about tiny amounts, such as having 5 grams of sugar from a teaspoon of honey in your tea... Small amounts of natural sugar like that is not a problem.

Sugar doesn't make your memory sweeter, it causes neuro degeneration, obesity, heart dis-ease, and tooth decay. Overconsumption of sugar and sugary foods can help you lose your memory, slowly but surely.

Obesity is the result of an energy imbalance, resulting from more energy (carbohydrates) consumed than used by the body, with the extra energy stored as fat. There may be other underlying causes for obesity, but many of them lead to comfort eating and excess sugar intake contributing to this imbalance. Therefore, it is important to increase your awareness of the presence of sugar in the foods that you eat.

Artificial sweeteners also feed sugar addictions; they keep your sweet craving going. There is also the issue of Aspartame in many artificial sweeteners and most if not, all diet drinks, which are very detrimental to your health if taken regularly. I call them MS in a bottle. If you must sweeten your drinks use Stevia, a natural sweetener, but just think how good you will feel once you break your addiction to sugar, sweets will lose their control over you, you will be in control and can then choose to have a little sweet now and then.

We often crave for a snack between meals, which most of the time is just a habit that you have acquired and can be changed. However, if this happens, try having a large glass of water or if you need more energy, try a fresh juice, or snack on fruit and vegetables, i.e. a carrot or celery stick, an apple, orange, banana or nuts instead of those sweet biscuits, cakes, doughnuts, and bread. It is important to read nutrition labels! Even foods disguised as "health foods" can be loaded with added sugars. Even some of those so-called 'Healthy smoothies' you buy in the Mall.

If you want to reduce your weight and/or optimize your health, I suggest you do your best to avoid foods that contain added sugars. The main foods to avoid, or class as treats now and then, are those with added sugar and sweets, beverages, ice cream, muffins, doughnuts, cakes & biscuits, processed and fast foods. Some people can handle a little bit of sugar in their diet, while for others it causes cravings, binge eating, rapid weight gain, and dis-ease. Every individual is unique and you need to figure out what works for you. If you are in the later mentioned I suggest that you avoid sugar completely, find healthy foods that you like, drink lots of water to flush your system and get plenty of exercises.

> "The doctor of the future…will give NO medicine,
> But interest his patient in the proper use of food,
> fresh air, and exercise."
>
> 'Thomas Edison'

My take on fats and oils

I have always looked at eating margarine as eating plastic, hence I avoid it. It is butter for me, especially living in New Zealand where we know that the cows are farmed on good pastures and will hopefully continue to do so.

I recently googled margarine and the first thing I saw was:

"And now, for Margarine"...

- Very high in trans fatty acids.
- Triple risk of coronary heart dis-ease.
- Increases total cholesterol and LDL (this is the bad cholesterol) and lowers HDL cholesterol, (the good cholesterol)
- Increases the risk of cancers up to fivefold.
- Lowers quality of breast milk.
- Decreases immune response.
- Decreases insulin response.

Then I clicked on a link that said "does margarine contain plastic" answer - Margarine is one molecule away from plastic, it was originally developed as an animal feed, to fatten turkeys and it increases cardiovascular-dis-ease risk – these are just some of the many claims made about margarine. (Report Feb 22, 2017)

Mmmm interesting, and of course those promoting margarine have conflicting reports.

When running healing classes or speaking to groups, I muscle test people to show how their energy is affected by different words, emotions, food, coco cola and cell phones. I have had margarine in a plastic container in my box of tricks for 18months or more. It hasn't gone rancid, nor does it smell. That alone tells me that it can't be good for you, especially if nothing will live or grow in it. The muscle testing with margarine always shows a negative, people cannot hold their power.

What concerns me the most is that the Heart Foundation gives many of these processed foods a big tick. Ouch!!

More interesting information...the difference between margarine and butter.

- Both have the same number of calories.
- Butter is slightly higher in saturated fats at 8 grams compared to 5 grams.
- Eating margarine can increase heart dis-ease in women by 53% over eating the same amount of butter, according to a recent Harvard Medical Study.
- Eating butter increases the absorption of many other nutrients in other foods...
- Butter has many nutritional benefits where margarine has a few, only because they are added!
- Butter tastes much better than margarine and it can enhance the flavours of other foods.
- Butter has been around for centuries, where margarine has been around for less than 100 years.

Many packaged foods are made with hydrogenated **vegetable oil** (HVO) which is one of the most health-damaging fats you can eat, if not worse than oxidized polyunsaturated fats according to one of the best books I have read with all of the facts and information on this subject - "Stop Alzheimer's Now" written by Bruce Fife. I recommend you read it.

Food scares are nothing new, but I take a lot of notice and research more when I read things like this - Hydrogenated vegetable oil elevates health risk to a whole new level. Recent scientific research suggests that it may be responsible for an unknown, but certainly very large, number of heart attacks.

Many people think that anything labelled as "vegetable oil" is good for you. Oh no! It's not even made from vegetables. Most of what is labelled as "vegetable oil" is simply heavily refined soybean oil (processed under high heat, pressure, and industrial solvents, such as hexane)… sometimes perhaps it may also be heavily refined cottonseed, safflower, corn, grape seed, or other oils too.

These processed oils in most instances are NOT HEALTHY for you. They are mostly composed of polyunsaturated fats (the most highly reactive type of fat) which leaves them prone to oxidation and free radical production when exposed to heat and light.

A New Zealand Physician, Biochemist, and Expert Nutrition author, Dr. Catherine Shanahan calls the fats in vegetable oils "Mega Trans", because they are similar in chemistry to trans fats but even worse. What is even worse is that they are in almost all processed packaged foods, as well as virtually ALL restaurant and takeaway fried foods.

Processed polyunsaturated oils are the most inflammatory when inside our bodies because of their high reactivity to heat and light. This inflammation is what causes many of our internal problems it develops such as heart disease, cancer, and other degenerative diseases.

The words hydrogenated vegetable oil is usually tucked away in tiny lettering on the ingredients label. It sounds harmless enough, but it is one of the most dangerous products ever that is in many foods we eat. Also, it is addictive, most foods containing it keeps calling you back to eat more, just like the sugar-added foods; once you have had one bite you want more. That's what the producers want, more sales, they aren't concerned about your health, they are more concerned about their pocket.

Do you value your heart? Please be aware that this isn't just a long-term risk of eating vegetable oils daily, the free radicals in vegetable oils also damage your arteries, which can directly lead to a **heart attack**. Some studies show ***immediate dysfunction*** in your arteries, also called endothelial function. (The endothelium is a thin membrane that lines the inside of the heart and blood vessels. Endothelial cells release substances that control vascular relaxation and contraction as well as enzymes that control blood clotting, immune function, and platelet (a colourless substance in the blood) adhesion).

Dr. Catherine Shanahan, M.D, in her book ***"Deep Nutrition"***, cites an interesting study that showed that subjects who ate French fries from a restaurant fryer displayed immediate harm to the endothelial function of their arteries, going from a normal 7% dilation before eating the French fries to almost NO dilation at all (only 1%) after eating the French fries. This is one thing that can cause a heart attack.

Dr. Shanahan also surveyed hundreds of patients that were admitted to hospital for a heart attack and discovered that every single patient that just had a heart attack had consumed foods made with vegetable oils with their last meal before the heart attack. Ouch!

Let's look at good fats:

MCT (Medium-chain triglycerides). This is clean fuel for mental & physical performance. Coconut-derived MCTs are easily absorbed and converted to ketones in the liver which help fuel the brain and body for mental and physical performance. Ketones allow the body to produce energy from good fats rather than from sugar and carbohydrates, hence it is an excellent low glycemic, ketogenic fuel to use for energy.

Coconut oil, has been a dietary staple of many civilizations for years and years, and it provides healthy, high-quality fat that benefits your health. Bruce Fife author of 'Stop Alzheimer's Now' calls it the ultimate brain food. The ketones that coconut oil stimulates your body to make are the preferred and more efficient type of fuel for your body to use. They are especially healthy for balancing blood sugar, boosts your metabolism, helps support healthy thyroid function, it is also good to help prevent Alzheimer's, and heart dis-ease. The MCTs in coconut oil are very easy for your body to metabolize and utilize immediately as fuel, making it an effective 'fat-burning' fuel, that doesn't raise blood sugar or insulin or stimulate fat storage. MCT's from coconut oil does not have to be broken down or semi-digested to be utilized by the body, unlike most other fats (Long Chain Fatty Acids) that do.

Saturated fats are the healthiest oils to cook with; they are much more stable in cooking conditions and less inflammatory than polyunsaturated oils with cooking. I use coconut oil; I have been eating it for years and will continue to do so in my smoothies, soups, stir-fries, roasting, in fact in all cooking. I even put it on my skin as a moisturiser; it is great to put on sunburn.

Extra Virgin Olive oil is okay for lower cooking temperatures as it's mostly monounsaturated, so it is moderately stable.

Saturated fats are more stable than monounsaturated and the least preferred polyunsaturated, which is not healthy.

So, use coconut oil or animal fats such as lard or real butter from grass-fed cows; not margarine.

Don't let deceptive marketing destroy your health.

I have come across some interesting studies recently on the relationship between coconut oil (or any type of coconut fat, including coconut milk and cream) and how it can affect your body fat... Research shows that Coconut oil is beneficial for your thyroid, brain, skin, oral health, heart health, detoxing, cancer, and more.

"Be the energy you want to attract"

Life Force Energy

Energy and your chakras	*174*
Fresh air and nature	*187*
Sunshine	*189*
The benefits of water	*192*
Exercise mind and body	*198*
Colour your life	*202*
Crystals	*205*
Toxins in your life	*208*

"The best and most Efficient Pharmacy is within your own system."

'Robert C. Peale'

Energy and your chakra's

We are all made up of energy; in fact, everything is energy. Your thoughts control the energy flow within and around you, whatever you think determines how you feel and what you experience.

Your thoughts are energy and are a major cause of dis-ease; negative thoughts can and will flatten the energy within your body. As

mentioned several times throughout this book, 'the words you use continuously and the pictures you create in your mind, create your life'.

Other influences on your energy are your beliefs, experiences, conditioning, energy from other people, what you eat, the exercise you do or not do, drugs and alcohol, your job, music, the sun and moon, crystals and colours, the list goes on. Each of these can affect your energy positively or negatively.

Modern-day pollution from industry, cars, electronics, sprays, and chemicals are major toxins that can deplete your energy, and without you realising it, cause dis-ease within your mind and body. On the other hand, good energy heals us.

When your energy is not flowing positively, your health is affected, you can feel sluggish, sad, irritated, angry, envious or jealous.

However, positive energy will leave you happy, energised, healthy, self-confident, positively enjoying life. Just like water flowing free of debris.

Your mind is so powerful and it will affect your energy, however, you **can** control it. It takes discipline, but you can do it. So, you need to do a check-up from the neck up regularly, monitor your thoughts and actions and adjust them if need be.

Let's talk about your body's energy centres.

Your energy centres are called "Chakras" which means "Wheel" (the Wheels of Life) in the ancient eastern language of Sanskrit.

Your chakra's, within and around your body are influenced by your thinking habits. In other words, the things you concentrate on most – Money, Spirituality, health, relationships, and so on, affect your energy centres positively or negatively, depending on how you think about them.

Although the body has many chakras, within, above and below, most people, including psychics and healers generally only concentrate on the seven major ones. Chakras push vital life energy through the body to ensure vitality. They radiate and receive energy constantly. They are circular vortexes of energy found next to hormonal glands deep within your physical body. Starting from your tail bone, and ending at the crown of your head. They are the focal points of your life force, (prana) and their individual states are vital to your holistic well-being.

If you hold negative thoughts your chakras can become closed or dirty with dense dark energy. Dirty chakras can't push through sufficient energy which leaves you feeling sluggish and out of balance. You can also lose touch with your natural psychic abilities and intuition.

Each chakra energetically relates to a specific sector, which 'governs' a particular area of your life. You have chakras for each issue that you commonly think about. There's a chakra related to thoughts about money & career, relationships, your future, appetite, lifestyle habits, goals & aspirations. Your thoughts affect the chakra that corresponds to what you are thinking about. This affects how you are feeling, positive or negatively. If you feel out of balance, you need to cleanse and balance your chakras regularly.

If you completely base your thoughts on love and faith, these chakras operate at a perfectly healthy rate, your energy, and life flow smoothly, you are happy and content. However, almost everyone is prone to worry or are preoccupied with their life's journey now and then.

Our chakra colours are the colours of the rainbow. Starting with the Base chakra - Red, Sacral - Orange, Solar Plexus - Yellow, Heart - Green, Throat - Sky Blue, Third Eye - Indigo, Crown - Violet.

You may need to ask a healer for help to open and cleanse your chakra's if you don't know anything about them.

However, once they are opened and cleansed you can maintain them yourself.

When open, your chakras spin in a clockwise direction. To spin, clear and maintain them, sit or lie, close your eyes and just imagine looking at a spinning disc or ball in the area of each chakra, one at a time starting with the lowest, which is your base chakra, it is red.

Now imagine filling it with the colour of the chakra (in this case red) and imagine spinning it from left to right. Your lower chakras spin slower than your upper chakras. If you can't see it or imagine the colour, that's ok, because where your thoughts go, energy flows, it will be happening. Spin your base chakra for a minute or so and then move onto the next, your sacral chakra, and continue all the way up to your crown chakra.

Because your chakras are now opened and you may not be used to your energy vibrating, I suggest you surround yourself with a bubble to protect yourself from any unwanted energies of others. When you are balanced and glowing, others feel your great energy and there is a chance that those with low energy may want to drain a little for themselves. So, protect yourself with a bubble of white light and you will be able to hold onto your great energy.

Just imagine it and it will happen.

The following is an explanation of each of your seven main chakras.

1. **Your Root Chakra:** This energy centre is associated with your root issues, such as your sense of security, satisfying your basic needs, familial relationships, and how at home you feel in your body and on this planet. It is responsible for your self-esteem and moving forward in life. It primarily influences your career, possessions, money mindset and your sense of belonging, survival and self-preservation instincts.

It can control the purely material aspects of your life.

Colour – Ruby Red

Crystals / Gemstones – Agates, Bloodstone, Garnet, Red Jasper, Obsidian, Onyx, Smokey Quartz, Rhodonite, Black Tourmaline, Gold

Sense – Smell	**Element** – Earth	**Glands** – Adrenal
Organs – Spinal Column, Kidneys, Bones	**Note** – C	**Planets** – Saturn, Earth

Location: Base of your spine (between your anus and genitals)

Variations of Energy- Grounded verses Disconnected. Security verses Insecurity. Sense of life purpose verses Aimlessness. Your ability to live on the physical plane.

If your Root Chakra is strong, open and in healthy alignment, you will be able to tap into its graceful stability to support a calm and steady energy. You will be in the state where you love your career and get rewarded for being so good at it. You always feel wanted, safe and loved by your friends and family, and you feel good about yourself when you look in the mirror, both physically and emotionally. Your needs are met. You are grounded, secure and have a sense of life purpose.

If your Root Chakra is weak, closed or out of alignment, you may find yourself busily bouncing from one thing to the next in a rush without appropriate attention or intention. Your physical and mental stamina will be low; this can lead to exhaustion, anxiety, and stress. On the flipside its imbalance can result in a feeling of lethargy, being stuck, feeling unable to take action, and manifest intention. You tend to get stuck in an unfulfilling and unrewarding career, and you never seem to have enough money, which leaves you worried and in debt. You may suffer from weight or body issues, which in turn leaves you feeling unworthy and uncomfortable, feeling insecure, lacking self-confidence. (life seems to be a heavy burden rather than joy)You live in a material structure that is not in keeping with your personality (work, home) You are likely to feel disconnected, insecure and have no aims. You tend to ignore the needs of your body (diet, health, rest). You don't pay attention to other's needs.

2. **Your Sacral Chakra** is the energy centre, the world of your emotions and feelings. It governs the relationship with the opposite sex, the ability to connect on an intimate level.

It controls the principle of giving and receiving on a physical level; digestion and metabolism on the emotional level; giving of yourself and accepting from others on a mental level.

Colour – Orange

Crystals / Gemstones – Agate, Citrine, Carnelian, Gold, Smokey Quartz, Tigers Eye, Pearl

Sense – Taste   **Element** – Water   **Glands** – Ovaries, testicles

Organs – Reproductive Organs – Internal and external, Thymus, Kidneys, Spleen

Note – D   **Planet** – Moon

Location: Lower abdomen (4fingers below the belly button)

Variations of Energy - Confidence verses lack of confidence. Ability to respond to verses Helplessness, Warmth verses Lust.

If your Sacral Chakra is strong, you see sex in a positive light, as a glorious, pleasurable and healthy activity. You enjoy physical pleasures – food, drink, sex, and thrill-seeking activities. You are able to attract the right partners and friends - compatible people who nourish you, fill you with joy and make you a better person. You have good exercise habits, sleep patterns, weight, health and thoughts about yourself and others.

If your Sacral Chakra is weak or closed, images of guilt and pain conjure in your mind when you think about sex. You rarely have the time or inclination to have sex, and when you do, it's mundane. You struggle to see yourself as 'sexy', and sometimes wonder how anyone could desire you. Your partners and friends are often wrong and incompatible with you. You often have bad obsessive habits and addictions.

3.  **Your Solar Plexus Chakra** is the seat of your personality. It is responsible for your self-esteem/self-image, vitality, and energy. It influences your personal power, your likes, and dislikes your social relationships. The ability to channel your personal power into the world, you receive validation of this from self and friends.

Colour – Yellow

Crystals / Gemstones – Aquamarine, Citrine, Carnelian, Golden Topaz, Emerald, Malachite, Tigers Eye, Smokey Quartz, Golden calcite

Sense – Sight   **Element** – Water   **Glands** – Pancreas, Adrenals

Organs – Nervous System, Liver, Gall bladder, Stomach   **Note** – E

Planet – Sun and Mars   **Location:** Three finger-widths above your belly button

Variations of Energy - Vitality verses Inertia. Inner Security verses Need to acquire and Attachment. Victor verses Victim.

If your Solar Plexus Chakra is strong, you are admired for your confidence and healthy self-esteem, both in your career and personal life. You have a self-appreciation and appreciation of others. You're never afraid to speak your mind, and you empower those around you to do the same. Your family, colleagues, and community see you as a charismatic individual, determined to use your charisma and power for making the world a better place.

If your Solar Plexus Chakra is weak or closed, you tend to struggle with self-esteem issues, and feelings of unworthiness. You have a poor self-image or hide behind a mask. You may need to dominate or exercise power over others or the opposite, be submissive.

You tend to question yourself when faced with important decisions; you don't believe what your brain is telling you to be true. You feel like a victim in the world, and often feel powerless to circumstances and other people's desires. You may also suffer from frequent stomach pains and stomach anxiety. In the absence of inner peace, you find it hard to relax.

4. **Your Heart Chakra** is the Chakra for unconditional Love, Relationships, Divine Manifestation, Self-acceptance, Compassion and Forgiveness, Validation of self and others. You radiate warmth and love to those you meet. It is here that the sensitive images, words, and expressions are transformed into feelings. This is where you perceive the beauty of nature.

The heart Chakra is a central component in the development of your intuition or clairvoyance, which means "clear feeling". The more we cleanse and open our Heart Chakras, the greater the intensity and accuracy our clairvoyance is. Circulation of our vitality socially and physically through the bloodstream.

Colour – Emerald Green

Crystals / Gemstones – Aventurine, Bloodstone, Carnelian, Emerald, Gold, Green Jade, Malachite, Moonstone, Rose Quartz, Pink & Green Tourmaline, Ruby

Sense – Touch   **Element** – Air   **Glands** – Thymus

Organs – Heart, Circulatory system, Lungs   **Note** – F   **Planet** – Venus

Location: Centre of the chest

Variations of Energy - Hope verses Arrogance, Self-esteem verses Vanity

If your Heart Chakra is strong, you enjoy comfortable, loving and empathic relationships at home, at work and in your community. You get along with your family. Your friends see you as a reliable person. At work, you're known as the one people can talk to. You feel a heartfelt sense of gratitude for how wonderful your life is, and feel compassion for all around you. You have a love for yourself and others and very forgiving. You will exude love, compassion, and vitality.

If your Heart Chakra is weak or closed, you tend to sabotage your relationships with distrust, anger, and a sense that you'll lose your independence if you rely too much on others.

You may struggle with commitment, experience frequent fights or misunderstandings with your loved ones, and always keep yourself "on guard" in case you get hurt by someone.

You may be too dependent on the love and affection of others, or you find it hard to receive the love of others, or you may feel you don't need the love of others

You are closed to your intuition. When conflict arises, you fail to stay calm and keep your distance, intellectually or emotionally

5.   Your Throat Chakra is responsible for your self-expression.

The Chakra of your "true voice," knowledge and purification, the identification and expression of your individual will, clarification of special needs and expression of this to others. It is the chakra for speech, communication & creative expression.

Thanks to the Throat Chakra, we can capture creative inspiration through the higher mind that drives us. Our thoughts are dominated by our feelings and physical sensations that prevent us from achieving objective knowledge.

Colour – Sky blue / Cyan / turquoise.

Crystals / Gemstones – Blue lace agate, Aquamarine, Fluorite, Lapis Lazuli. Sodalite, Blue Topaz, Turquoise.

Sense – Hearing   **Element** – Ether   **Glands** – Thyroid, Parathyroid

Organs –Throat   **Note** – G#   **Planet** – Venus

Location: Throat- below Adam's apple

If your Throat Chakra is strong, you are good at voicing out your thoughts, ideas, and emotions to those around you. You're admired for your willpower and strong communication skills, and your conviction to speak the truth, even if it may be uncomfortable to some. Your career and personal life are enriched as a result. You find it easier to communicate via singing, writing, speaking and teaching other people.

If your Throat Chakra is weak or closed, you have communication problems or difficulty expressing yourself clearly, fear of talking about your ideas, feelings, beliefs and showing weakness or strength. You constantly feel like nobody cares about your opinions, and that you have nothing of value to say. You're likely to be known as the 'quiet one' in your professional and social circles, and you frequently settle with following other people's opinions. You're afraid to change. You often suffer from a blocked and sore throat. Communication channels are closed or tainted.

6.  **Your 3rd Eye** is your Intuitive Chakra, formless consciousness, the psychic and intuitive sense. The intuitive insight that transcends the five body senses and the limitations of time and space, extrasensory perception. This Chakra acts as your inner compass for thoughts and feelings, the power of positive thinking. Connected to the ability to visualize and perceive mental concepts, imagination.

Colour – Indigo blue.

Crystals / Gemstones – Blue lace agate, Amethyst, Aquamarine, Lapis, Turquoise. Sapphire, Fluorite

Element – light – mind   **Glands** – Pineal, Pituitary   **Note** – A

Organs – Activates the nervous system   **Planet** – Jupiter

Location: Centre of the forehead, between the eyebrows

If your Thrd Eye Chakra is strong, you will be able to master the power of positive thinking. You can make accurate intuitive decisions and evaluations about your career, your family and the intentions of other people. You often know things without knowing exactly how you know them, and you have a clear sense of direction and clarity in everything that you do. You have a vivid picture of where your life is headed, and the people around you are likely to rely on you for guidance and advice. Good visions of past and future and positive spiritual beliefs. Your 5 senses will be heightened– See, smell, taste, hear & touch

If your Throat Chakra is weak or closed, you tend to feel helpless or lost when faced with decisions and judgment calls. You may have a block in creating ideas. You are non-assertive, indecisive, uncommitted and have a lack of confidence with the decisions you end up making because you have a history of making the wrong ones. Afraid of success, ability to generate strong negative ideas or have egotistical pride, manipulative or religiously dogmatic. You feel spiritually lost, and your true purpose is unclear to you. You often get headaches and feel the tension in your brow area. You have fears from the past and of the future.

7. Your Crown Chakra influences your connection to the divine, feeling of oneness. It is the Chakra of divine consciousness.

The spiritual urge and the desire to experience the wholeness of life and the universe. Inspiration and revelation of the higher self. Self-realisation and enlightenment. The receptor for incoming cosmic rays. Integration of whole being – Physical, emotional, mental and spiritual.

Colour –Violet Purple

Crystals / Gemstones –Amethyst, Citrine, Diamond, Gold, Clear quartz, Silver, Topaz.

Elements – Cosmic energy, thought   **Glands** – Pituitary, Pineal

Organs – cerebral cortex, right eye   **Note** – B   **Planet** – Uranus

Location: Inside the top of your head

If your Crown Chakra is strong, you perpetually feel connected to a higher power, be it God, Universal consciousness or simply your higher self, a sense of alignment with higher forces. As you go through your daily life, you are always reminded that you are being watched over, and you feel immense gratitude for the universal love and appreciation you feel towards yourself and others. Others describe you as "glowing". You will have stimulated inspiration, higher consciousness, wisdom, and understanding.

If your Crown Chakra is weak or closed, you tend to feel little or no connection to a higher power, and always feel alone with little or no spark of joy. No conscious sense of one's spirituality or a constant sense of frustration. You have unrealised power. You may feel like you are being told what to do. You feel unworthy of, or disbelief, in spiritual help, or perhaps even angry that your higher power has abandoned you. You often suffer from migraines and tension headaches.

Don't worry if your Chakras are weak or closed in certain areas! It's called being human ☺ There is help out there to open you up and clear you of negative energies.

The rest of this chapter looks at some of our energy-enhancing or depleting everyday occurrences.

"Everything is energy;
Your thought begins it,
Your emotion amplifies it,
And your action increases the momentum".

Fresh air and nature

To maintain a healthy life, you need plenty of fresh air. It is imperative that you get out into nature as much as possible; preferably barefoot to ground yourself. Take in one of nature's best energisers, "fresh air", take a walk on the beach, by a lake, river, or in the bush. As you do breathe consciously, slowly and deeply into your abdomen with a smile on your face and feel your energy change.

Many people are working in air-conditioned shops and offices, some work with toxic substances, paint, sprays and vehicle fumes. Working or playing with modern technology is also very toxic to our body with EMF (Electro Magnetic Frequencies) all around. Working on a computer all day can play havoc with your eyesight as well as deplete your energy. So, take time out regularly throughout the day, stretch and twist your body every half hour, even if it is only for 30 seconds. Yawning will also get oxygen into your system if you are feeling tired working at the computer or concentrating hard on paperwork. Get outside as much as possible. If you aren't near a lake, river, beach or native bush there is usually a park nearby, if not, as you walk to turn on your imagination, pretend you are at the beach, in native bush, or wherever you enjoy nature.

As you walk, taking in that beautiful fresh air, be aware of your surroundings, feeling the energy from nature. Walking barefoot on the beach or grass will help ground you, taking in the energy from the earth, trees and flowers. If you take a walk on the beach, feel the energy of the rolling waves. Listen to them, and breathe with them as they go in and out. Or find a trickling creek, a flowing river, or one of my favourites is waterfalls. Feel and listen to the flowing water. This is a great way to ground and energise yourself; to balance your mind, body, and energy.

Wherever you are, stop for a few minutes, breathe in the fresh air, use your awareness, all of your senses; see, feel, smell, taste, hear to what is around you; the sounds and activity of the birds, the rustle of leaves, laughter of children playing, dogs barking. Be aware and soak up the amazing energy of nature.

I am so lucky living in New Zealand, with fresh air and nature so readily available, I can be at a beach, lake, river, and mountain all within one day, at the most only three hours apart. I love and embrace the beauty of nature every day that I can.

"Life is like a cup of tea; it is all in how you make it"

Sunshine

Can you imagine being called a Ray of Sunshine and a Winner? Talk about building one's self-esteem. Well, when travelling, I am often asked my name, as you do, and as Raewyn is not a well- known name outside of New Zealand, it takes people a little while to get it. So, I just say its Raewyn just think of a Ray of sunshine and a Winner and you will remember it, and they do. It is a great ice breaker and makes me feel good; like a bright sunny confident person.

Sunshine is one of our best energisers, so my advice is to get into those rays, that brilliant healing sunshine, for at least 10 minutes on your bare skin each day when possible. Catch the sunrise and or the sunset rather than in the heat of the day. At this time, the sun will not burn and you can stay in it longer, up to 20 minutes. But don't sun gaze, that's a little too hard on the eyes.

The energy of the sun is so amazing because sunshine is an incredibly powerful healer and it plays a major role in your overall healing, providing so much more than just vitamin D. It is so beneficial for your whole wellbeing. Let's face it, what on earth would be alive without it.

The suns energy can lift your spirit; it helps alleviate depression, anxiety, fear and panic. The sun can change your life. It's a miracle at your fingertips and it is free, so soak it up and enjoy it.

According to the University of California, San Diego, researchers determined after analysing cancer deaths and sun exposure that Vitamin D could help reduce the risk of 16 types of cancer by anywhere between 2 to 70 percent.

According to Healthline.com, the Sun Is Your Best Source of Vitamin D. There's good reason why vitamin D is called "the sunshine vitamin." When your skin is exposed to sunlight, it makes vitamin D from cholesterol. The sun's ultraviolet B (UVB) rays hit cholesterol in the skin cells, providing the energy for vitamin D synthesis to occur.

If you haven't got the sun, just try closing your eyes and imagine you are lying in the sun, feel the warmth, feel the sun's comforting rays filling you with life-force energy. Can you feel it? It almost feels like someone is hugging you.

If you need to take vitamin D supplements, take vitamin D3 as it is the best according research. Anthony William, Medium Healer, says: "The truth is that the sun enhances every single vitamin and mineral within us equally. Why we chose just to pick up vitamin D, it's kind of odd when the truth is that vitamin B, vitamin C, vitamin E, every micronutrient, every mineral, selenium, molybdenum, zinc, copper, every single mineral in you is enhanced by exposure to the sun just like vitamin D is."

He goes on to say "There are millions of people that don't get sunlight on their skin ever in their lifetime and have lots of skin cancer to battle and deal with. More so with people who avoid the sun than people who get sun. So, we can't be afraid of skin cancers or we're going to cheat ourselves of the ability to enhance all the healing properties the sun offers."

I have the belief that the chemicals in most sun prevention lotions will do more damage than the sun. I have not used it for many years and do not have a problem with the sun, as I am sensible when it comes to exposure. I wear sunglasses and a hat and don't bask in the sun. (Although I did in my younger days.) We just have to be sensible about how long and when we soak up those rays. They will burn if you are in the mid-day sun for too long.

There is so much research on sunlight (The sun, sun-beds and tanning beds) and how they cause cancer. However, if you take a responsible stance and don't soak in the sun for hours in the heat of the day, your health will benefit from sunlight.

The Sun will help reduce depression and energize your day if you:

- Expose yourself to the light of the rising and setting sun.
- Spend more time outside during daylight.
- Let as much natural light into your home or workspace as possible.
- If necessary, use a Sun box (Light Box Therapy)
- Stay close to people that feel like Sunshine

"Happiness can be found even in the darkest of times only if one remembers to turn on the light."

'Albus Dumbledore'

The benefits of water

"As we strive for a happier and more fulfilling life, we can draw a lot of inspiration from water. Despite being soft and humble, it cuts through hard rocks because of its patience and persistence."

Water is a conductor of energy. Good drinking water is crucial for health and well-being. Unfortunately, many people do not consume enough each day. Over 60% of your body, 90% of your blood and 70% of your brain is water and we must drink plenty of good quality drinking water to stay hydrated, avoid headaches and help flush out toxins.

Water is the most important beverage for us to survive. We can survive for weeks together without food but without water we may not survive for more than 3 to 5 days in most cases.

Water is needed by all organs and organ systems of the body for their optimum working. Water is needed right from hydrating the body to the transportation of nutrients to being involved in a lot of chemical reactions going on in the body, to name a few.

Therefore the importance of water to our well being cannot be over emphasised.

Many think because they are consuming fluids like soft drinks, tea and coffee, that they can count it as drinking water; not so. Tea and coffee are good in small doses, one or two a day, however, they actually dehydrate your body. As for soft drinks, they are so full of sugar, ouch, as you would have read in my take on sugar previously, it is a no-no.

Practitioners of Chinese Medicine believe that drinking warm water that is around body temperature, maintains a healthy balance. They believe **that** *extremes of either hot or cold throw off the body's yin and yang.* These imbalances are believed to be responsible for symptoms like chills, depression, thirst, "foggy" thinking, sleepiness, bloating and more.

Water isn't just "good for you" — water helps to burn fat; it suppresses hunger and renews your skin. Just drinking 12 plus ounces of pure water every day can take a few years off your face in a matter of weeks. You'll also drop fat, have more energy, and save your kidneys and liver from chronic overwork.

The consumption of water is so necessary, here are more benefits:

- **It prevents kidney damage -** The kidneys regulate fluid in the body. Insufficient water can lead to kidney stones and other problems. When your kidneys are taxed from too little water, your liver has to take over, which takes it away from all of the other great work it has to do.

- **It forms saliva and mucus -** Saliva helps us digest your food and keeps your mouth, nose, and eyes moist and clean. This prevents friction and damage

- **It delivers oxygen throughout the body -** Blood is more than 90 percent water, and blood carries oxygen to different parts of the body.

- **It boosts skin health and beauty -** It helps prevents skin disorders and premature wrinkling.

- **It lubricates the joints -** Cartilage, found in joints and the disks of the spine, contains around 80 percent water. Long-term dehydration can reduce the joints' shock-absorbing ability, leading to joint pain.

- **It cushions sensitive tissues throughout the body, especially in the brain and spinal cord -** Dehydration can affect brain structure and function leading to problems with thinking, memory, and reasoning. It s also involved in the production of hormones and neurotransmitters.

- ➢ **It regulates body temperature -** Via sweating when the body heats up. As it evaporates, it cools the body.
- ➢ **Your digestive system depends on water -** Dehydration can lead to digestive problems - acidic stomach leading to heartburn, stomach ulcers and bowel issues such as constipation.
- ➢ **And of course there is your body's sewage system -** Water is needed to flush out your bodily waste through sweating, urine, and faeces.
- ➢ **It helps maintain blood pressure -** A lack of water can cause your blood to become thicker, causing high blood pressure.
- ➢ When dehydrated, your **airways** become restricted by the body to minimize water loss. This can make asthma and allergies worse.
- ➢ Drinking water before meals can help prevent overeating by creating a sense of fullness helping with **weight loss**.

Drinking hot and cold water has different effects and consequences within the body.

Here are a few impacts of drinking Cold water:

- ➢ If you have been exercising and are extremely hot, you can shock your system, possibly even inducing a heart attack. The body's natural temperature is 37 degrees Celsius. Also, when you drink something very cold, your body has to spend an exorbitant amount of energy to regulate your core

- temperature. This takes away from energy that is needed to digest food and absorb nutrients.
- Extremely cold water may cause respiratory issues, possibly causing a sore throat.
- When consumed, water goes to the brain first, it can alleviate headaches, however according to studies undertaken; women who had experienced a migraine in the last year were twice as likely to trigger a headache by drinking cold water.
- Drinking cold water with ice can be detrimental as in many countries the ice can be contaminated, or if your ice maker is not clean it could contain bacteria.
- Drinking any water during a meal will dilute your saliva, slowing down your metabolism, and cold water is said to promote the hardening of oils and fats in the food, leading to a fat deposit in the intestine.

So, forget cold water, try drinking hot and warm (room temperature) water is so beneficial.

- **Warm water boosts your metabolism** and aids the digestive process, not recommended with a meal, preferably at least ½ hour before and after. It helps with weight loss **and helps to** flush compounds from the body that can accelerate aging **and aids in cellular repair hence improve** skin elasticity.
- Hot water is a great natural treatment for colds. It naturally dissolves phlegm and clears your airways; it clears out nasal and throat congestion and soothes sore throat symptoms as well.
- Drinking warm water **breaks down fat deposits that are present in the body and bloodstream.** The warmth increases

- ➢ the flow of blood circulation and promotes the removal of toxins. The increased circulation induces muscle relaxation, which can reduce pain.
- ➢ Warm water can **provide pain relief**
- ➢ Drinking warm or hot water has a **soothing effect on the muscles of the abdomen. It** can provide relief from menstrual and abdominal cramping, as well as muscle spasms.
- ➢ Hot water can finish breaking down food remnants and flush them through the intestines, **hence it helps prevent constipation and helps you maintain bowel movement regularity.**
- ➢ The act of drinking hot water naturally raises the temperature of the body; it **helps detoxify your body.** As the body temperature rises, it activates the process of sweating, which **flushes toxins out of the body through the pores of the skin.**

Good hydration helps the function of the kidneys to flush waste material out of the body, along with toxins.

Here is a little bit of information to ponder – According to Dr. Michael Wald, New York, "consuming hot water activates receptors found in the stomach, oesophagus, intestines, and mouth. This stimulates pleasure regions of the brain".

And did you know that "Each day, we lose a little more than a cup of water (237 ml) when we exhale" and "Water regulates the Earth's temperature"?

For many years now I have drunk **lemon water** every morning, ½ hour before eating to help hydrate, detox and alkalise my body. Your body becomes dehydrated overnight and your liver has been working hard gathering and removing toxins from your body so it needs to be flushed. By adding Lemon juice to water, it activated it which helps it to remove toxins from your body.

Yes, lemons are acidic, but they have an alkalising effect in the body when digested. Even though I have the juice of ½ a lemon, if you haven't got a good supply, using just 1teaspoon of lemon juice, per 8-ounce glass of water will help you, just not as effectively for a good detox. Eating foods that are alkalising can be an additional way to increase the benefits of drinking alkaline water.

Lemons contain citric acid, magnesium, bioflavonoid, vitamin C, pectin, calcium, and limonene, which supercharge your immunity so that the body can fight infection. They help to lower the activity of free radicals and increase the breaking down of body fat supporting weight loss; Lemons promote hydration, improve your skin quality, aid digestion, freshens your breath and help prevent kidney stones.

For over a decade, I have followed an old Hawaiian tradition, Ho'oponopono. I energize my water by fusing it with the healing power of the sun. I put good drinking water into blue glass bottles with a non metallic lid and place them in the direct sunlight for at least 60 minutes.

Wow! It's a must, say 'yes' to a cup of good clean warm or hot water or lemon water.

Honour the flow of life – Drink water

"When life throws obstacles in your way, be like water and either cut through them or form a new path that will lead you to your goals and dreams".

Exercise mind and body

When you exercise your body your mind benefits, when you exercise your mind your body benefits, you feel fitter, healthier and generally better about yourself, hence your self-esteem rises.

Please, don't tell me that you don't have the time or money for exercise. We all have 24 hours in the day, I say organise them, get your priorities right. You can exercise free of charge, the old saying 'everything good for you is FREE'. There is no need to go to a gym, however many need to, for motivation. It is certainly a lot cheaper than having to go to the doctor regularly.

When most people think of exercise, they tend to immediately think of super intense forms of exercise that take it out of you. While this type of exercise can be good and can help you go that extra mile with your health, it's simply not needed. If you find you don't have the energy to engage in those types of sessions or you simply aren't at the fitness level to do so, this doesn't mean you can't reap great benefits of less active exercise.

If you don't work out at all, you're going to lose muscle tissue every year. That means you'll get fatter and flabbier with less shape and more sag.

The same goes for exercising the mind, if you are not creating new neuro pathways and keeping your mind active, it will slowly weaken. Is this what you desire? If yes then that is your choice, however I can't imagine so.

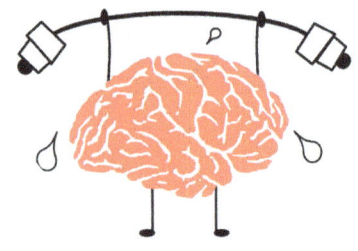

You may have a dog that will let you know if you haven't taken them for a walk, having a dog is kind of like having built-in accountability. No matter whether it's a pet, a partner or friend who walks or rides a cycle with you, or you do it alone, it doesn't matter, just do it. Do something to make sure that you are moving that body, getting out in fresh air (if possible) and getting energised.

Exercise not only benefits your whole body, but it is also very beneficial for your brain, it will help improve your memory and concentration.

If exercise is new to you, it is never too late, start small and grow your time and energy with your exercise. The fitter and healthier you are the more energy you have, the better you will feel, it reduces stress, which means you can concentrate and get more things done.

You are in control; you have choices in life. 30 minutes of brisk walking (2 steps per second), per day or at least 5 days a week is a good aerobic workout. Exercise your lungs by breathing slowly and deeply; regular yoga, Tai chi or Qi Gong are also great for the mind and body.

Being a couch potato is not an option. There are many free videos online that you can get guidance and learn from. If you are confined to a wheelchair or bed, you can still stretch, twist, exercise your eyes for eye health, deep breathing, tap or cup your body all over from head to toes, where ever you can reach, move your arms and legs, whatever will move, you need to get your bodies systems flowing. No excuses. My sister who had both legs amputated used to get on the floor and exercise every morning, and laugh about it if anyone was around. Check out the 'Daily Routine' in the exercises and Remedies section at the back of the book.

If you are fully able-bodied, walking, dancing, going to the gym, doing sports such as tennis, squash, table tennis, badminton or swimming, are a few suggestions. If you are unfit, start with 10mins walking 5 days a week and work your way up to 30 then 60, if you feel like it.

The more you energise yourself, the more your body and mind will want it. Keep in mind what I talked about in chapter 4, your body likes what is familiar, so it might resist at first. Make exercise familiar, you are in charge, you have choices.

If you are feeling stagnant, depressed, overweight or simply just uninspired to move your body, remember you have a choice. You can stay uninspired and unhealthy, or put your mind or body into gear. Regular exercise will help you feel good about yourself, it will raise your self-esteem, you will have more energy, your partner and friends will love you for it and your body will be healthier. Movement gets your body's systems going and will put you on a healing path.

If you do choose to buy a membership to a gym, remember you have to use it for it to be beneficial.

Posture is another big influence on how you feel. Try sitting or standing with your shoulders rounded and a frown on your face, how do you feel?

Now, sit straight, shoulders back, chin in, take a big breath in, now how do you feel?

Now put a smile on your face and notice how much better you feel again. Notice how your stomach looks slimmer too when you stand up and lower your chin a little, it pulls your torso up and tummy in.

Over the past few years, I have gone dancing, mainly Rock 'n Roll, between one and four nights a week, played table tennis or badminton off and on, swim in the sea, walk or cycled at least five days a week. Every morning I do 15 minutes of passive Qi Gong and energy exercises, use a power fit machine for 10 minutes and do other stretch and floor exercises. I often break out into dance if the right music comes on and time permits, it's fun. However, if I miss a day, I don't beat myself up, two days and I start questioning myself and my motivation.

I know that exercise benefits me, keeping me young in mind and body. I am not saying this to boast, I want to help you; I want you to be healthy and shine too. I understand that you may not be able to or even want to dance or play a sport, but there will be something out there you will like doing that will energise and benefit you. I want you to know that I don't ask anyone to do something I won't do myself; I walk my talk and am healthy because of it.

"It's all about mindset.
Yours!!!
"From the moment you wake up, to the moment
you go to bed at night.
Everything is up to you.
Your emotions, your thoughts, your perceptions, your reactions.
Every moment"

Colour in your life

Colours have been used for healing for many hundreds of years. The effect colour has on human life is phenomenal. We are so blessed to be living in an era where people have an understanding of the power of colours and their effect on human life.

Colour plays a major role in setting up and controlling your mood, emotions, feelings, and state of mind. Many businesses use specific colours which respond to the nature of work they do and to sell products. Multi-national companies conduct a lot of research and even engage Colour analysts to know which Colours to use in their advertisements and promotional campaigns. Colours tend to send a subliminal message to our brain which can be the root cause of success or failure.

All planets correspond to specific colours, so it is not surprising that colours play a very important role in Astrology too. For example, the planet Mars is red, Jupiter is yellow, Mercury is green and Venus is white and so on... Nature is full of colour, the trees, flowers, plants, rocks, shells, mountains, valleys, sea, and sky, along with every man-made thing.

We talked about our bodies' energy centres, our main Chakra's and how they relate to specific colours – the colours of the rainbow. Red, Orange, Yellow, Green, Blue, Indigo and Violet.

Colours can either soothe or irritate us. The medical fraternity has confirmed that colours can raise blood pressure and even upset our appetite. Wearing colourful clothing can make you feel alive and fabulous or dowdy colours may depress you.

Colours are a form of communication: red is considered a power colour, we also related red to stop and hot and green for go or as in our heart chakra it means love, pink is also a colour of love. Many different colours are healing.

It is interesting to note that everyone has personal opinions about colours. There are always colours which we like more than others and some we don't like at all. Everyone has their own favourite colour/s. My mother, when she saw a yellow car always said she hated them, yet she wore yellow. I always liked yellow cars; they stand out; mind you I like most colours and wear a great variety.

I remember when I was a district councillor, the Mayor (male) at the time asked me not to wear my lovely red suit in council. He was obviously intimidated by it.

Many years ago, I studied Quantum-Touch healing. Through this, I learnt that every cell in your body is made up of 12 colours and if you are deficient in any of them it will affect your wellbeing. It always fascinated me and I have used this information and colours along with the colours of our chakras for healing ever since.

The following information is from Alain Herriott's book "Supercharging Quantum-Touch":

Six Inner Layers Govern the Function and Maintenance of the Body.

These colours are: **White** which is your life-force energy

Violet carries the part of your being called spirit.

Indigo facilitates communication between spirit & body

Metallic Copper governs the neurological and cardiovascular systems within your body.

Metallic Silver governs the bones, teeth, tendons, muscles, cartilage and nails.

Metallic Gold governs the functions of all of our organs, glands, soft tissue, skin, hair and eyes.

Six Outer Layers Govern our Personal Empowerment.

These colours are:

Yellow which holds the vibration of internal alignment which brings you the deepest sense of well being

Emerald **Green** supports the emotional body in matters of Self-love, self-worth and self-esteem

Cyan helps you to speak your deepest truth It aligns your thoughts with your heart or your emotional self and supports integrity

Blue (Deep rich sky or sapphire blue), vibrates harmonically with creative thinking – **Magenta** contains the wisdom and compassion that encompasses love

Mother of Pearl is the outer most layer and is equivalent to the protective blanket that you would wrap a new-born in.

These cell colours all relate to and can heal different organs within the body.

Another good source I recommend to learn about the power of colour is Inna Segal's books "The Secret Language of Colours" and "The Secret Language of your Body"

Make every day colourful and your life will be colourful, take time to enjoy the colours, and take time to smell roses.

> "Life is like a box of crayons"
>
> John Mayer

Crystals

Crystals have amazing energy and many healing qualities; they come in many forms and colours. They have the power to free up energy blockages, re-establish, purify, heal, ground and harmonize your energy.

There are crystals for happiness, joy, love, relationships and much more. The following are a few popular crystals to give you an idea of the power and properties crystal can hold and be used for.

One of the most used crystals is **Amethyst**, its healing properties are plentiful, it is thought of mostly as a protective stone. As it is linked to the crown chakra, it helps you connect with your higher self, purify your mind and clear it of negative thoughts; this includes the negativity  of stress and anxiety, which is why many meditate with amethyst ridding them of that darkness. It is a good overall crystal that can help with healing, soothe emotions, sleep and your general environment. It is good to have under your pillow at night, or carry in your pocket if you have an ailment. Despite its prevalence, amethyst has been one of the world's most revered stones for many centuries. Ancient Greeks and Romans used amethyst in several ways from beads in jewellery to amulets. These ancient civilizations placed a high value on this stone. They believed that the amethyst crystal meaning was synonymous with luxury.

Rose Quartz has been used in love rituals and ceremonies for centuries. It is considered the Love magnet with properties to promote unconditional love, compassion, happiness, forgiveness, and peace. This stone will open up your heart chakra to every kind of love that you need—whether it's self-love, familial love, friendship love, love for humanity or romantic love. Rose quartz will assist you in releasing toxic emotions so your spirit can finally be free of petty negativity.

Agate is a stone of strength and courage; it tones and strengthens the mind & body, grounding and stabilising emotions and physical energy. It helps with increased concentration and confidence, agate makes it easier to focus on what is good in your life, so that you can heal from mistakes and bring harmony to everything you do.

Blue Lace Agate will help you if you have a fear of public speaking and fear of confrontations. It will help you to speak your truth, soothe anxiety and calm your spirit.

Citrine energizes the solar plexus chakra to radiate power, centeredness, confidence, and endurance. It is one of few stones that, rather than absorbing negative energy, clears it, a great cleanser. It makes room for happiness and light so the spirit is open to positive possibilities.

Bloodstone will get your blood pumping and revitalize your energy with a surge of courage, self-esteem, energy, and protection so that you can enjoy living in the now. It is a stone of both physical and creative movement and stimulates the root chakra helping to get the energy flowing in your mind, body, and spirit.

If something always seems to go wrong in your relationships, **Malachite** can cleanse the chakras and bring you to a realization about what's not working. It's one of the most powerful transformational crystals for the heart. It provides an emotional balance that encourages you to take action to remove negative patterns and transform.

Smoky Quartz is a crystal that will elevate your mood and help you remain balanced in any situation. Smoky Quartz helps you to overcome negative emotions such as stress, fear, anger, jealousy, and even feelings of depression. It absorbs electromagnetic energies.

You can buy crystals in various forms, shapes, and sizes. You may be drawn to purchase a certain crystal. If you are requiring a crystal for a certain purpose there is plenty of information on the internet or ask your retailer for assistance, they are generally good for advice.

s soon as you buy a crystal, purify it in cold running water for a few minutes. Rivers or water falls are good, if not available cold water from a tap will suffice. Then put it in the sun for an hour or two. If using you crystals for healing, ensure to cleanse them under running water after each use as they may have absorbed negative energies. Placing your crystals out under a full moon will also energise them.

Refer back to the previous section on chakras to see what crystals relate to the different chakras, and the particular organs they aid.

> "When you can't control what is happening.
> Challenge yourself to control the way you respond to what's happening.
> That's where your power is."
>
> 'Buddha'

Toxins in your life

Toxins are in our life; we can't get away from that. Given the right environment and TLC, your body can normally deal with most toxins in moderation. However, with the increase of toxins around us these days, we do need a little or a lot of help at times.

So, what do we consider toxic? Mostly we think of toxic emissions, fumes, and substances, but think about what you have been reading in this book. There are toxic relationships, food, drugs, thoughts, memories, substances, chemicals, plants, environments, EMF, mould, even songs. The list goes on.

We have addressed many of them and the internet can address many more for you. I just want to bring your awareness to the many toxins that can affect your mind and body, toppling your energy off balance.

Your mind and your brain are two different things and can be affected in different ways. However, when your brain is affected it also has a major impact on your mind and body.

- ➢ You can detox your mind by being aware of your words, thoughts, the pictures you create in your mind and catching those ANT's. And what I consider a real biggy, is getting away from toxic relationships and watching the foods you eat (remember that sugars and bad fats and oils can slowly affect your mind and body significantly).

- ➢ You can detox your brain by eliminating drugs, cigarettes, and excess alcohol. Alcohol and drugs severely eat away at your brain, let alone your mind, some more than others and I don't need to tell you what nicotine does to your lungs. Beware of inhalants such as gasoline, paint thinners, glue, etc., Consuming too much caffeine (More than three cups a day) and nicotine, even though they temporarily enhance your mood, they are dangerous to your brain health.

- Mercury is a major toxin which affects your brain and body. 2500 years ago, it was thought to be good for us all and a concoction of mercury was given to everyone that was ill. Then in the 19th century, it was deemed a dangerous toxin to anyone that came in contact with it according to Anthony William in his book 'Medical Medium'. He says that Mercury is a top fuel for cancer, viruses and bacteria. He states that Mercury has injured or killed well over a billion people. It has taken people through Alzheimer's, Parkinson's, dementia and strokes. The main ways we take in Mercury are seafood, including fish oil pills, and dental amalgams. If you have concerns, Anthony's book has amazing stories and cures.

- As for your body, there is a myriad of detoxifying options out there, especially in the dietary field; however, it is best not to pollute yourself in the first place. Prevention is better than cure. So, limit your time on phones and computers, wear preventative clothing or equipment where necessary.

- Working with sprays, paints, glues and loud noise are all very toxic and can affect the health of your brain and eventually your body.

Here is an interesting insight into the Brain Wave Warping Effect of Mobile Phones:

According to Sayer Ji, Founder of GreenMedInfo.com, a study reveals that your mobile phone is not only a carcinogenic, radiation-emitting device, but may alter the structure and function of the brain, including brain wave activity that is intimately connected to cognition, mood, and behaviour. A concerning clinical study published in ' PLoS One' titled, "EEG Changes Due to Experimentally Induced 3G Mobile Phone Radiation," has revealed that so-called third generation (3G) cell phone technology has widespread brain wave disrupting activity in subjects exposed to real-world like conditions, i.e. 15-minute "talk time" exposure to the ear area.

He goes on to say "Even though it is now common knowledge that cell phone radiation is powerful enough to disrupt sensitive equipment within an airplane (think: airplane mode) or hospitals, there is still resistance to acknowledging it may adversely affect the human brain, an electrical impulse sensitive organ. Moreover, since brain waves are believed to encode rules for behaviour, altering brain wave activity could have considerable downstream effects on behaviour and consciousness." It's scary stuff huh!

A few suggested solutions to help with toxins in your life:

> I recommend you check out information and books of Medical Medium, Anthony William, his books are "Medical Medium" and "Liver Rescue."

 I believe these books will answer any questions and give many solutions considering that the liver is usually the first organ to be affected with toxins, even toxic relationships, as anger affects your liver intensely.

 These books address and have answers to Eczema, Psoriasis, Diabetes, Strep, Acne, Gout, Bloating, Gallstones, Adrenal Stress, Fatigue, Fatty Liver, Weight Issues, SIBO &Autoimmune Disease. He has helped tens of thousands of people heal from ailments that have been misdiagnosed or ineffectively treated or that doctors can't resolve.

Anthony in his book "Medical Medium" also talks about toxins that are passed down from generation to generation causing ADHD and/or Autism in young children. The great thing is he gives solutions. He says "Toxins are not behind ADHD and autism, the body does not attack itself, blaming DNA blames the very essence of the child who suffers ADHD and/or Autism and that's a shame. The reason that ADHD and/or Autism sometimes run in a family is a generation to generation transfer of mercury, as well as family patterns of exposure to toxic heavy metals".

He goes on to say "It's easy to be exposed to the other toxic heavy metal typically involved with ADHD and Autism. Most soda cans are made of aluminium, aluminium foil is a popular item in the kitchen, and aluminium siding is common in homes. Aluminium and mercury show up in pesticides, fungicides, and herbicides, too. This is a big eye-opener for many.

- There are many brain experts across the world. One I recommend is Daniel Amen M.D, a clinical neuroscientist who I have mentioned several times throughout the book. He has helped thousands of people and has many books on regaining your brain. He talks about and shows how toxic, chemicals, substances, even relationships, slowly kill your brain and how to turn it around.

- Don't spend too many hours on your computer or phone researching; they too are toxic if held close for too long.

- Use your common sense and intuition, your body and inner self knows what is good and safe for you. And be aware of the toxic people in your life. Toxic relationships are one of life's biggest stressors, causing Dis-ease.

➢ Avoid toxic foods – Sugars, processed foods, fast foods.

"The gut is the seat of all feeling.
Polluting the gut not only cripples your immune system,
but also destroys your sense of empathy,
the ability to identify with other humans.
Bad bacteria in the gut creates neurological issues".

'Unknown Author'

Relationships

What happens after the honeymoon?	214
Know your love language	216
Choose your friends wisely	218
Loneliness is a major issue	221

"I used to think that the worst thing in Life would be to end up alone.
It's NOT!
The worst thing in Life is to end up with people who make you feel alone"

'Robin Williams'

What happens after the honeymoon?

So what happens after the honeymoon period is over?.... married or not.

Relationships are just like the seasons. When you start your relationship it is springtime and everything is bright and wonderful, you have a spring in our step and your heart.

Then you get married, or you live together for a year or two and summer begins, it is still lovely and warm with great activity.

Then autumn kicks in and finally winter.

If you don't put the spring back into your relationship, you may get stuck in winter and that's when things can sometimes go awry. You may be cosy, but it can get a little boring or even go a little mouldy. Once the mould sets in, if you are unable to clean up your act and bring the spring back into the relationship, that's when things go horribly wrong.

If your love bucket is empty, your zest and enthusiasm are slowly lost. Just like your bank or self-esteem account, you need to keep topping it up if you want to keep it prosperous and able to draw on it.

The desire for romantic love in a partnership is deeply rooted in our psychological makeup. To be able to communicate and keep your love alive in our relationship you need to know and speak your partners' emotional love language.

Once you identify and learn to speak your partners' primary love language, I believe that you will have discovered the key to a long-lasting, loving relationship.

A partnership is a two-way street, both need to consider each other and both need to be happy.

If your relationship is not working, fix it, communicate and work it out or get out, were the words I heard many years ago from Don Tolman, 'whole foods and healthy living Guru'. It shifted my butt. Communication and honesty are the name of the game. Bad relationships, whether with a spouse, partner, family or friends, are the quickest thing to stress you, if you allow them to. Toxic relationships cause dis-ease, one way or another.

Many people, women in particular stay in a dysfunctional relationship thinking that change will be more painful than staying. This often comes from past conditioning or fear of the 'what if's'.

Holding onto unhappy relationships causes so much dis-ease, it creates angry, sad, stressed, suppressed, confused, sick people. Everyone needs a positive supportive friend or network that they can talk to, and have a positive attitude and outlook on life with.

Life is meant to be lived joyously, happily, healthily, sharing good energy with partners, family, and friends, laughing, singing, dancing, relaxing and playing games with, whatever floats your boat.

So start taking personal responsibility for your life and your relationships. You may surprise yourself, your life will flourish as you take your power back.

"If you are willing to look at another person's behaviour toward you as a
Reflection of the state of their relationship with themselves
Rather than a statement about your value as a person,
Then you will, over a period of time
Cease to react at all."

'Yogi Bhanjan'

Know your love language

To help people identify their Love Language, Gary Chapman wrote the book – "The Five Love Languages". I would recommend every couple buy this book and read about each love language. Not knowing each other's love language, or even knowing that we had one, was one of the main problems, along with a lack of communication that broke my marriage of 38 years. We all have a primary love language, however most of the time we treat people how we like to be treated and think that they should be happy. Unfortunately, how we treat others is usually what we love, our love language, which is not necessarily theirs.

The Five Love Languages are:

> Words of Affirmation
>
> Quality Time
>
> Receiving Gifts
>
> Acts of Service
>
> Physical Touch

If your love language is physical touch and your partners love language is receiving gifts, a gift won't do it for you. The gift may be nice, but what you really want is regular hugs, you need touch, intimacy. Your partner will not understand why you aren't so excited about the gift because he/she loves them because that is their love language. Touch doesn't necessarily mean sex all of the time. If your love language is touch and you are not receiving the hugs you crave, you will more than likely be switched off by your partner and not want sex anyway. Likewise, if you don't give gifts to your partner they are going to be switched off.

If words of affirmation are your love language and you never get thank you, you did well or look good, once again you will slowly shut down. It is not your partners' fault, he or she won't know your love language unless they are switched on and have read and understood your love language. I encourage you to get the book.

There are also books to identify the love languages of children and teens. It could save you a whole lot of anguish through misunderstanding. You may think you already know your primary love language. Then again you may have no clue, don't try to guess it as you could be completely wrong.

Communication is the name of the game. We come from ancestors that lived in tribes and community is so important to everyone. We all like to feel that we belong and are loved. That is why many people go astray and join gangs, or link with a church or other social group, we need to feel wanted and part of a family.

> "Life is the most difficult exam.
> Many people fail because they try to copy,
> Not realising that everyone has a different paper."

Choose your friends wisely

Ensure that your friends are positive people that contribute to your happiness. Choose 'victors' as friends, as opposed to 'victims' who will drain you and clutter your mind with negative stuff.

It's important to acknowledge the power of positive thinking. This goes not only for yourself, but also for the people you surround yourself with. Attitudes are catchy. Whether they're positive or negative, they're rubbing off on you.

If you surround yourself with people who complain, judge, spread negative gossip, blame others, and play victim roles, chances are you do, too. (ouch!)

Have you heard the saying "if you want to know who you are, take the 5 people you spend most of your time with and put yourself in the middle"? Yes, that is you. This can be scary, a real eye-opener. Yes, we become like the people we spend most of our time with for better or for worse. So hopefully the 5 people you spend the most time with are happy, positive, healthy people, if not start to make changes, look for better friends.

You have to take responsibility for this area of your life. Look around you at the people you call friends. Does it make you feel good, proud? Are you selling yourself short? Or are you on the right track? Keep positive people around you and you will be much happier, healthier and motivated! Be around people who can accomplish their goals and you will accomplish yours, too! The choice is yours to make. Are the people around you achieving their dreams or complaining about their circumstances? Do they look up to others who are go-getters and high achievers, or do they make fun of them? How do they treat you?

If you're spending time with people who don't support you, your dreams and goals, it's seriously time to look at who you call your friends!

Make a decision to take control of your life. You will feel so proud of yourself and have so much more energy as you are not wasting it going around in circles and feeling that you have to please others. Be decisive, do a check-up from the neck up regularly and clear that brain, prioritise and take action. Keep lists and use your diary, keep your brain clear of clutter and you will think more clearly and feel so good about life. Live in the moment and be aware of what or who is ruling your life.

Imagine going on a holiday with a good friend with just enough clothes for a relaxing, fun time, leave your phone and computer behind, watch no or limited TV, have a good book to read. No one can contact you unless it is an emergency, in such a case a message can be left at a number of the place you are staying which you have only given to selected people. You have nothing to do except enjoy yourself. How does that feel?

I can just hear some of you saying – 'my mind would not switch off from what has to be done'. Well here is a real-life story to show what happens if you don't take time out.

Many years ago, my husband and I decided to go on a cruise for our 25th wedding anniversary. We asked another couple to come with us as it was their 25th anniversary one week before ours. The husband said he was too busy; he was building a house. I could see that he was stressed and tried to convince him that a holiday would be good for him, but no, he was too busy. A few months later he had a stroke, in his late 40's, he is now in his 70's, has not worked since, still coping with paralysis and now stuck in a wheelchair. Not to mention the stress he put onto his wife and family over all of those years. My husband and

I still went and had fun, but what fun we could have all had together, and our friend would most probably still be healthy. He wasn't thinking of his wife either, for a relationship is a two-way street.

It is not worth it; stress is the major cause of dis-ease and pressure on relationships.

We have relationships with ourselves as well as others. How do you treat yourself? Do you put yourself first? You need to be number one in your life, refer to the section on Self-esteem. Get to know the inner person you are spending all of your time and energy with; do you really know yourself? Do you like who you are?

We have relationships with our parents, siblings, children, friends and each relationship will be different. Each relationship will thrive on a different kind of love, vibration, energy. You will treat your baby, your children different from your partner or parents. Each will have a different personality and love language.

Here is food for thought; It is always good to remember that life is a mirror, it reflects and gives back what you give out. So, wouldn't you want to give love, joy, laughter, peace, forgiveness, gratitude to everyone in your life, including yourself?

> "None of us has the power to make someone else love us.
> But we all have the power to give away love, to love other people.
> And if we do so, we change the kind of person we are,
> And we change the kind of world we live in."
> "Life is as good as your mindset"

Loneliness is a major issue

You can be lonely when you are in a marriage, a relationship, with family or on your own. If your relationships are unhealthy you can be and feel so alone, especially if you have not got the motivation to do your own thing or move on. Your motivation can be stifled by put-downs by your partner or others; lack of communication, little or no understanding of each other's needs or love languages.

You could have lost a partner through death after a long happy marriage, or through separation or divorce and not be able to cope on your own. The separation or divorce may not have been you're doing, you may have thought that your relationship was going well, not realising that your partner was unsatisfied. This may put you into a real slump, feeling lost and lonely plummeting your ego and self-esteem leading to stress, loneliness, and low self-esteem. Especially in later years loneliness can lead to the onset of Alzheimer's and other dis-eases of mind and body. If this is so you need help. Talk to family and friends if you can, they can most probably see what is happening and be able to help. If family and friends are not an option then get professional help. My advice is if it's not working, communicate with your partner, family and try to fix it or get out.

If you have a mother, father or sibling in their later years and living alone, please check on them regularly to ensure they don't go down this path.

Life is too short to be unhappy or to stay in a rut, which by the way is the definition of a coffin with its ends knocked out.

"Happiness is a choice, not a result.
"No person will make you happy unless you decide to be happy.
Your happiness will not come to you; it can only come from within you".

'Ralph Marston'

Music and Meditation

The benefits of music 224
Heal with meditation 228
Take time to relax 233

> Plato said music is moral law:
> "It gives soul to the universe, wings to the mind, flight to the imagination, a charm to sadness and life to everything."

The benefits of music

I love music; it is in my blood and is the first thing that goes on in the house in the morning that is of course after I have opened the curtains to let the sunshine in. Music energises me, it takes me back to my younger days, and it brings back great memories of times, places and people. On the other hand, if I want to meditate 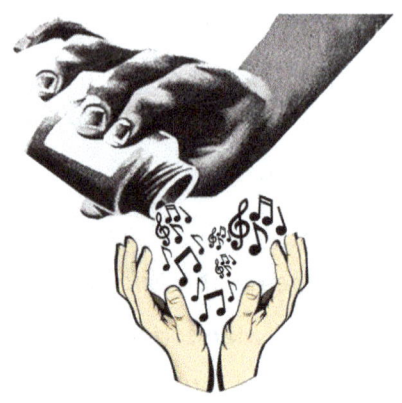 or go within, I put on appropriate meditative music. Music can take you to where ever you want to be, if you go with it.

Henry Wadsworth Longfellow called music the "universal language of mankind."

I have been a healthy living motivational presenter in Mumbai, India working with Roshan Mansukhani who calls himself "A Simple human. Roshan is a DJ; he uses music as a holistic healer" doing amazing work with many teenagers and adults transforming them from addictions to healthy living.

One thing is certain; music has the power to transform lives. Mediator and peace-builder John Paul Lederach say's **"Music is especially effective in helping traumatized victims heal from unspeakable violence, injustice, or war**. Music, among other things, is based on sound, and sound is based on vibration". He told public radio's Krista Tippett, host of **'On Being'**. "Vibration touches us", so the way we experience music is much more holistically." Lederach, a pioneer in conflict resolution, said: "Violence numbs people, in healing a lot of it is about feeling like a person again, and music permits that to happen in a much deeper way".

Scientists tell us music literally moves within us. Music travels through the brain's auditory cortex directly to the limbic system, the part of the brain responsible for emotional responses, hormonal secretions, motivation, pleasure, and pain.

Music helps the left and right brain work together more harmoniously and productively. It activates the flow of stored memory and imagined material across the bridge between the left and right hemispheres.

Music also excites peptides in the brain and stimulates the production of endorphins. Endorphins are sometimes called "natural morphine," because they are opiates we produce naturally to elevate our mood.

Studies have shown that listening to music reduces chronic pain and depression in people suffering from arthritis and other conditions… it calms premature babies, increasing their suckling rate, leading to weight gain, it lowers blood pressure and generates feelings of well-being.

When a song evokes a memory so vivid you feel like you're back in that place and time, you experience music's transformative power. I do this daily with the radio station I put on as soon as I get up in the morning. The station plays music from the 1950s to the 1980s, the years I grew up. It takes me back to my childhood, teenage years and early adulthood. It has me dancing and singing. I love it. In my community, many go to Rock n Roll lessons and dances, both the young and old and the energy generated, the laughter and fun are so energising. Not to mention the exercise we are all getting in both mind and body, as learning new steps is amazing for our brain.

Music can also program your mind, so you need to be mindful of the music you and in particular your teenagers, listen to all of the time. Many songs are sad, talk of war, lost love, sex, drugs, and some full of swearing and foul language, so make sure you are listening to beneficial, happy, uplifting music, or if need be meditative, relaxing and healing.

We learn, as our mind is programmed by repetition, so be aware of what you are listening to regularly. I often find myself walking on the beach, singing a song that I love the tune of, but all of a sudden realise that the words aren't very positive, so I change the words and use the tune. Try it, it can be fun.

When I left my Husband in 2008, I decided I needed to empower myself, lift my self-esteem and move on in life. I found a great song "Dare to Be" which was so inspiring. It was written and sung by humourist, songwriter, and educator Jana Stanfield who combines laughter, wisdom, and her million-selling songs into an interactive experience that generates fun and positive action. Here are the Lyrics:

I've come a long way, down this road
Always learning as I go
But you can't look backward, and get ahead
It's time to lead and not be led

Chorus

Goodbye limitation
Hello liberation
Goodbye frustration
Hello to living my life by my design
Breaking these chains that bind my mind
Learning to colour outside the lines

Dare, dare to be, dare to be
Dare, dare to be, dare to be Unconventional

Repeat Chorus two more times replacing Unconventional with 'One of a Kind' then 'You' the last chorus

I still love and sing this song as I walk down the beach.

What kind of experiences do songs evoke for you? Does music play prominently in your life today? Do you sing in the shower? or on the beach? Do you worry about what others think of your voice?

I always used to say, "I have a beautiful voice but there is just a rough passage for it to come out of". I was married to a very good singer for many years and felt my voice wasn't good enough even though he asked me to sing with him at home parties. I have always loved singing but never felt good or confident enough to let loose and just sing when I felt like it, until the last 10 or so years. I love singing now and don't really care what anyone else thinks. I go with the old saying "don't worry be happy."Actually, that is a song too. What others think is none of my business. This is yet another lesson on self-doubt, self-esteem, and programming.

Music can help you manage stress; it can take you to another world whether through meditation, just listening, singing or dancing. It is all about doing what you like to do, taking charge of your life: taking charge of your thoughts, your emotions, your schedule, your environment, and the way you deal with problems. Most importantly, enjoy music, allow it in your life to help you heal.

"Music expresses that which cannot be put into words and That which cannot remain silent"

'Victor Hugo'

Heal with meditation

Sound, especially for healing, relaxation, and meditational purposes, has become popular in the last few decades, although it has been used for healing and prayer for centuries, especially in Asian cultures. 'Om' is considered a very sacred mantra in Hinduism and Tibetan Buddhism. It appears at the beginning and end of most Sanskrit recitations and prayers and many spiritual people and groups use the sound for healing. Many other sounds are often chanted, which is repeating a sound in a monotone or repetitive way, during healing, prayer, in churches and other groups, during meditation or healing.

I learnt when studying with Master Chunyi Lin, of Spring Forest Qi Gong, that certain sounds have profound healing effects on different organs and systems of the body.

Different music and sound frequencies are now being used to mend DNA, for cell regeneration, miracle skin repair, to help get you into certain brainwave states for deeper meditation. This to me is mind-boggling; a lot to get one's head around, but it is working.

You may be sceptical or asking, what is meditation? Many think that they have to sit for hours in a cross-legged position and hum Om. If that's what you want you can, however, it is not necessary. There are different ways to meditate.

Meditation is proven through many studies around the world to be so beneficial for your mind and body. Since meditation helps you live in the moment, it helps you block your thinking and sensory input, which can, in turn, help you ease stress, anxiety, and worry.

Meditation can even help you achieve what is called brain synchronization, which is the ability to use both sides of your brain together.

Stress reduction is one of the most common reasons people try meditation. It will help your emotional health and enhance self-awareness.

It is also said to lengthen your attention span and even help reduce age-related memory loss, help fight addictions, control pain, decrease blood pressure and improve sleep. Wow, so many benefits. There are many free meditation MP3's on the internet these days, guided meditations or just music.

Take the time for yourself to ground and balance your energies. If your energies are out of alignment your life will be unbalanced.

The main goal of meditation is to relax and calm your "monkey mind." That constant and restless shifting of thoughts that goes on in your head all day. Did you know that we have 70,000 to 90,000 thoughts run through our heads every day and the interesting thing is that 90% of those thoughts are the same day after day? Practicing mindfulness meditation helps to quiet the thoughts clamouring for your attention and to direct your attention to one thought or sound that serves as your "anchor." Your anchor could be the sound of water flowing, the repetition of a word, or even your breath.

A simple way to go into meditation is to sit or lie, any way you want, there are no rules, although a straight back is preferable. It is best to close your eyes, but once again not necessary, take a few deep breaths and feel what is happening within your mind and body.

You can do this for any length of time and just go within, take your awareness inside your body, try it.

When thoughts come into your mind (and believe me they will), simply try to dismiss them.

To dismiss a thought and try to get back to focusing on your anchor, simply observe the sensation of the breath entering your nose, feel the cool air entering your nose and filling your lungs, and then feel the warmth of it being released through your nose. As thoughts come into your mind, try to dismiss them and get back to focusing and observing your breath.

You may find that a single and pressing thought keeps reoccurring. If that's the case, take the time to ponder why that thought is so important right now. Ask things like "Why is it returning? Is it important? How does it affect me? How can I effectively deal with it?"

This is focused-attention meditation, where you concentrate your attention on a single object: focus on breathing, a mantra, a calming sound, a thought, or visualization. The emphasis is on ridding your mind of attention and distraction.

Awareness meditation encourages you to focus your awareness on all aspects of your environment, train of thought and sense of inner self. Becoming aware of your thoughts, feelings or impulses that you might normally try to suppress.

Once again you can concentrate on the cool air in your nose as you breathe in and feel the warm air as you breathe out for a few minutes; this takes your mind away from thinking. Put your hands on your lap or over your heart space and just imagine that you are breathing in through your heart, remember, where your mind goes your energy flows, put a smile on your face and feel how you feel inside. I find this a simple but amazing experience and every one I get to do it with me just loves it. You can sit with this for as long as you like, it is great to do as you drift off to sleep.

To relax, you can do a full-body meditation, starting with your awareness on your feet. As you breathe in tighten every muscle in your feet, hold it for a moment, then relax your feet as you breathe out. Move on up to your calves, thighs, buttock, spine, stomach, chest, shoulders, hands, arms, neck, face, and scalp. Then relax your whole body, put your hands on your heart, a smile on your face and breathe in through your heart space, release as you breathe out and either go to sleep or get up feeling relaxed but energised. You can play relaxing music if you choose.

There are so many meditations to help you with relaxation, healing, going to sleep, programming your subconscious mind; you name it you will be able to find what you need on the internet.

Taking a walk in nature, on the beach, in the park taking in the ambiance of nature, the sights, sounds, and smells are also a type of relaxing meditation. Stop and smell the roses.

Drop the guilt of sitting and relaxing, read a book, play a musical instrument, spend time with animals, watch a movie, do some sort of hobby, artwork that relaxes you.

Give your mind and body time to catch up with its self if you are a busy person.

Gee, I think I need to take a little of my own medicine here, I don't blob out very often and when I do, I often think I should be doing something constructive. One of my favourite sayings to clients and friends is "Don't 'Should' on yourself or others, just do it", Mmmm I am pretty good most of the time but I guess I too am human and slip up now and then, so just at the moment I think I had better take my own advice and relax more often.

You know your life is balanced and stress-free when you can take things in your stride and say 'well it just is'. I take the view that if there is nothing I can do about it then there is no point in worrying or stressing over it. If I can change it then I think what I need to do to make the change and then take action.

Life is crusier when it is stress-free☺. I am working hard to complete this book, that is where my 'should's' are coming into play.

If you learn to relax, love and look after yourself, you can then and only then, have the ability to love others or can expect others to love you? Be selfish in a loving way, love yourself for who you are, live by your values and you will be more comfortable and relaxed with yourself and others.

Start your internal love engine. Put a smile on your dial. Chunyi Lin of Spring Forest Qi Gong teaches that Smile is the acronym for '**S**tart **M**y **I**nternal **L**ove **E**ngine.'

> *"Love is free, give it to everyone and every living thing, including yourself"*

> *"Life, he realised, was much like a song.*
> *In the beginning there is mystery, in the end there is confirmation, but it's in the middle where all the emotion resides to make the whole thing worthwhile."*
> *'Nicholas Sparks', The Last Song*

Take time to Relax

There is not enough time to do what I want, what I love to do, time for me, for my family and friends, to go to the gym, for a walk before work, and on it goes, does it ring a bell?

Time is what most people complain that they don't have enough of.

We are all given 24 hours per day; 'if it is to be it is up to me,' make time.

In reality, man-made time, once upon a time it didn't exist. So, try it for a day, take off your watch, put your phone away and give yourself a day off. Eat when you're hungry and sleep when you're tired. Slow down enough to be able to tune in to your real self, with nature.

Discover who you are, what you need and what works best for you. The way you spend your time is the way you spend your life.

Think about it, when you are doing what you love, time flies, you forget about time. When you are with someone special, listening to the music you love, creating something, painting or volunteering, you have to agree, time just flies by.

Whether you like it or not, the clock keeps ticking, so live your life fully, every single second of every single day. Live in awareness. Learn the true joy of doing less and having more as you experience each day. Fill your life with as many precious moments and experiences of joy and passion as you can.

Time is more important than money, once you have spent it you cannot get it back. Spend your time wisely.

When you find yourself doing something that doesn't serve you, you can choose to change it, and if you do you can change your life. Do what you love and take time for you. Time waits for no one so use it wisely. Work smarter not harder. Remember you are a human being not a human doing.

However, to get yourself to relax just do it, I find the easiest, most beneficial way for me is to breathe consciously, be aware, take long, slow, deep, breaths with my eyes closed and a smile on my face. Try it.

*"A Diamond is a piece of coal under pressure,
If you are feeling pressured today you are about to shine"*

Sleep

The Importance of quality sleep 236
Tips to help you sleep better 240

"The people who get on in this world are the people who get up and look for the circumstances they want, and if they can't find them, they make them."

'George Bernard Shaw'

The importance of quality sleep

It is so important that you make good quality sleep a high priority; you need as much as you can. So why, you might say, "I can do a day's work with just a few hours!" or "I can party, watch TV, play games until early hours in the morning and then catch a few Z's! I have done it for years and I survive!"

Yes, you might survive, but that will be all. Your body will tell you so after a while too if that is how you are treating it.

A good night's sleep is imperative, it is essential for a healthy mind and body. It is when your body heals and your brain recharges and resets itself. It's also when your memory gets consolidated so that you can recall it later on down the line. If you're someone who typically suffers from poor memory, it could be due to too many nights of not enough or broken sleep.

The advice from sleep experts couldn't be clearer. If you have trouble sleeping, seek help. Ignoring the problem increases the risk of high blood pressure, diabetes, heart attack, stroke, poor memory, depression and Alzheimer's dis-ease. The experts advise you to seek out natural sleep aids, saying a visit to the doctor's office too often means a prescription for sleeping pills. Even if the pills give you a better night's sleep, it's a type of sleep that may not decrease your Alzheimer's risk, and the drugs themselves may harm your brain if taken long term.

You are spiritually recharged during sleep. Adequate sleep is essential for joy, vitality and healthy living.

Michael Breus, PhD. aka 'The sleep doctor,' says in his book 'The Power of When' – "In the last 15 years scientist have been connecting the so-called diseases of civilization (Mood disorders, heart disease, diabetes, cancer and obesity) with chrono- misalignment (chrono means 'time'). Symptoms include insomnia and sleep deprivation, which leads to depression, anxiety, and accidents, to say nothing of what feeling overwhelmed and exhausted does to relationships, careers and health."

He goes on to say "unless you turn off every screen and light at 6pm, you are likely to deal with chrono- misalignment in one way or another, whether it's morning fogginess, extra weight, feeling stressed out, or not performing to your potential. (It's unrealistic to power down at dusk, of course. But you can turn off screens a bit earlier than usual and dim lights as night goes on)."

According to Maria C. Carrillo, PhD, Alzheimer's Association chief science officer, "Research has shown us that not getting enough sleep because of insomnia or sleep apnoea may result in problems with memory and thinking, and increase the risk for Alzheimer's-related brain changes." "The new findings reported at AAIC 2019 are important because disrupted sleep patterns not only put the overall health of people with dementia at further risk, they may also worsen their memory loss and disrupted thinking."

Focus on not only sleeping more but getting higher quality sleep by setting a good sleep environment. Turn down the temperature in your room, block out inconsistent noises (such as passing cars), and make sure that your room is as dark as possible. This will help ensure that you get the best quality of sleep so you wake up feeling well-rested.

Are you having difficulty catching some Zzz's? Are you so worn down, feeling that you could sleep for a week, but your mind won't switch off? It's driving you crazy!!

Its 3:00 am, you wake up and still half asleep make your way into the bathroom, two minutes later you come back and slide into bed and all of a sudden, your mind, which had been happily snoozing away just two minutes before, starts thinking. Now, apparently with great urgency, your mind decides you need to worry about a meeting you've got tomorrow; how you're going to deal with a team member who is not doing their job, you start stewing and regurgitating a past mistake, pondering over something someone said to you that you didn't like; you name it, silly things start running through your head, crazy. You're thinking "really"? What the heck was that about? It's 3:00 am and I should be sleeping…

Does this sound familiar? Of course, it happens to the best of us, maybe not every night, but it happens regularly enough to bug you.

You need to take control of that overactive mind. An overly active mind late at night is one of the BIGGEST things keeping many people from falling asleep.

Declutter your mind before you go to bed and tell yourself that you are going to have a great night's sleep right through the night until you need to get up.

Eliminating the use of devices, computers, emails, and any other work related to your job (or other stressful things) at least three hours before you plan to go to sleep is a must. Using devices or computers for casual reading is fine for up to 1 hour before bedtime, but don't do any work that gets your mind overly activated. Keeping your eyes focused on the light from devices is one thing that some researchers are saying could interfere with getting quality sleep.

One trick that works for many is to grab a book, choose a topic that you find a little "boring", it will take your mind away from other things that are going around in your mind and will help you to fall asleep. Any book helps me drop off to sleep easier.

"Each night, when I go to sleep, I die.
And the next morning,
When I wake up, I am reborn."

Mahatma Gandhi'

Tips to help you sleep better

1: Support your body's natural rhythms

- Try to go to sleep and get up at the same time every day.

- Avoid sleeping in—even on weekends.

- Limit naps to 15 to 20 minutes in the early afternoon.

- Do something; read, play a game (not electronic), chat with your partner, to help fight after-dinner drowsiness.

2: Control your exposure to light

- Avoid bright screens within one to two hours of your bedtime.

- Say no to late-night television.

- Be smart about e-readers.

- When it's time to sleep, make sure the room is dark.

- Keep the lights down if you get up during the night.

3: Get regular exercise and you will sleep better

4: Be mindful of what you eat and drink before going to bed

- Limit caffeine, maybe a cup of Chamomile Tea or Cocoa (not sweetened chocolate) at least an hour before bedtime

- Avoid big meals at night.

- Avoid alcohol at least two hours before bedtime

- Avoid drinking too many liquids in the evening.

5: Wind down and clear your head

- As you lay in bed do some deep breathing.

- Maybe some calming music and a little meditation as you go to sleep.

- Relax your muscles progressively.
- Visualize a peaceful, restful place.
- Ensure your room is dark, cool, and quiet

6: Ways to get back to sleep.
- Stay out of your head.
- Concentrate on relaxation rather than not being able to sleep.
- If wide awake do a quiet, non-stimulating activity for a while.
- Avoid worrying and thinking about what needs to be done. If you are a worrier have a pad and pen by your bed, write down whatever is keeping you awake, then put it aside knowing you won't forget it.
- If you are worried about sleeping in, suggest to your subconscious mind prior to going to sleep the exact time you want to wake. And it will wake you.

7: Try using crystals.
- Amethyst is a quieting stone for those enduring fatigue due to emotional overload. This purplish crystal is ruled by the component of Air and the planet Jupiter. It's thought of as an awesome healing stone for emotional weariness, insomnia, and headaches. Place it under your pillow or bed.
- Rose Quartz will likewise bring a more relaxing sleep if placed beneath your pillow. It is also a quieting stone that will greatly help with an overtaxed brain and bouts of insomnia.
- Blue Lace Agate will help you relax, if held in your hand it will help your entire body relax.

Here is another interesting fact - lack of sleep can make you GAIN weight?

It is essential to have a proper hormone balance, for both reducing fat, and keeping it off.

Lack of sleep, through restless sleep, going to bed too late, getting up too early, or any other types of sleep deprivation can throw your body's hormones out of balance.

So regardless of what type of diet you go on or how much you exercise you do, you will still struggle to reduce your excess fat, especially from your stomach, if you are deprived of good quality sleep.

However, if you don't have a good night's sleep, don't be mad at yourself, or get up grumpy. Tell yourself you have had enough sleep and are going to have a fantastic day. It works I have been doing it for years. Have a nana nap in the afternoon if need be.

Here are some suggested night time affirmations to say as you are about to go to sleep:

I am Calm and Peaceful

I have done my best today

My mind and body are relaxed

I am proud of myself

I am grateful for my achievements today

My heart and mind are strong and peaceful

My mind is at rest

Thank you for the great opportunities the day has presented

I breathe in peace and breathe out unwanted energy

Life is amazing

Sleep

I am safe, happy and abundant in every way

I am filled with contentment and gratitude

I am now ready for a peaceful, healing, sleep

Your Life is the Creation of your Mind

Sweet dreams

"Be the energy you want to see in the world
Give yourself the same care you give to others"

"Buddha"

Muscle Testing

What is muscle testing? **245**
Can I muscle-test myself? **247**
Using a pendulum **249**

"Belief increases the magnetic attraction of your thoughts.
If you are merely sending your thoughts out, with no belief
attached, it's like casting your fishing rod with no bait attached
to the hook. BELIEF is HUGE"!

'Fred Ford'

What is muscle testing?

Muscle testing is a practice that is used to tap into the subconscious mind to answer questions about physical, mental, and emotional well-being. It's a non-invasive method that can be used to determine the underlying causes of ailments and afflictions an individual might be suffering from, identifying everything from nutritional needs to trapped emotions.

Our bodies live and function on principles of bio magnetic (the phenomenon of magnetic fields produced by living organisms) energy. While our conscious mind is mostly oblivious to these energies, our subconscious mind is intimately connected to and affected by them. They are responsive to positive energy and similarity, and they are resistant to negative energy and dissimilarity. It is this tendency to seek out or reinforce positive energy and to avoid or refuse negative energy that allows us to perform muscle testing.

We tap into this relationship between the subconscious mind and energy by asking "true/false" "Yes/no" questions and then checking the body's response. Checking the response can be done a number of ways, but is often done with methods like the Arm Test, where the person simply holds one arm outstretched in front or to the side of them, parallel to the floor.

The tester then places two fingers on the person's wrist, and asks a question, placing a small amount of pressure on the wrist. If the subject's arm resists, that is a "strong response," and it equates to a "yes" answer. If the arm gives way under the pressure, that's a "weak response," and equals a "no" answer. This strong response/weak response is the basis of muscle testing and is what allows us to get answers to help the recipient.

What your mind says yes to, your body says yes to.
What your mind says no to, your body says no to.

Can I muscle test myself?

If you are in-tune with your body and believe, you can also perform muscle testing on yourself, using the same principles.

The Ring Fingers Test is the most frequently used, where you make interlocking rings with your forefingers and thumbs. When you ask a question, you gently attempt to pull the rings apart, attempting to separate them. Resistance (the rings staying together) indicates a positive answer. If you can't hold your fingers together (the rings breaking apart) it indicates a negative response.

There are several different ways to utilise muscle testing. This is another simple one: Stand straight, balancing yourself upright with your hands at your sides and ask yourself a question. Let your body "hover" and let it fall in the way it wishes. If you tilt forwards it's a 'yes.' If you tilt backwards it is a 'no,' if you don't move, you need to ask a better question, or it is neutral.

To test if anything is good for you or not, e.g. a food, vitamins etc., you can do the last test yourself. Hold the product or object in one hand against your solar plexus and ask the question, is this beneficial for me? Once again if you tilt forwards it's a 'yes.' If you tilt backwards it is a 'no,' if you don't move, you need to ask a better question, or it is neutral.

With any muscle testing, for an accurate answer, wait for at least three seconds after you have asked the question before you test for the answer. This allows your subconscious mind to get the question.

There are a few common issues that may interfere with your ability to muscle test yourself or others.

Muscle testing requires a certain amount of faith and trust, trust that your inner self can help you determine what ails you or your patient. Trust and just know that your subconscious mind knows the answers and that if you are performing the test properly, you will be able to interpret the response correctly.

You need to make sure you ask a clear question and wait a second or two for it to be recognised.

Dehydration can have several negative effects on the human body, including the ability to muscle test. You will find it difficult to get an accurate response if either the person you are muscle testing or your own body is dehydrated.

Applying too much pressure as you test can also interfere with results, possibly giving you inaccurate testing. You need only a nominal amount of pressure to determine a strong or a weak response.

You can also experience difficulty muscle testing if you are suffering from misaligned neck vertebrae, if you are dealing with certain trapped emotions or other difficulties that will make you less receptive to positive energy.

"Insanity: Doing the Same Thing Each Day and Expecting Different Results!"

Using a pendulum

As well as muscle testing, I frequently use a pendulum; I love and trust it immensely. Using a pendulum is a little bit the same as muscle testing and a good way to develop your intuition. It's not a gift - anyone can learn to do it! It is a simple technique through which you can receive psychic and inner guidance, you get yes, no or ask a better question response to just about anything from relationships, food, career, life situations. You name it; you can get accurate responses.

A pendulum is a weight attached to a string or chain; it can be a crystal, a rock, anything that is not too heavy or too light. There is nothing magical or physic to using a pendulum

The body responds to truth with power and non-truth with weakness, this can be easily demonstrated with muscle testing, and just as in muscle testing, the body responds with a yes or no, true or false when using a pendulum.

To begin using a pendulum you need to identify what a yes or no response is. So, when I get a new pendulum, I program it, I move it in a circular motion from left to right and say "this is a yes response". Then I move it back and forwards and say "this is a no response". Then I move it in a circular motion from right to left and say - this response means "ask a better question."

Then I test it by keeping my hand very still and asking the pendulum to give me a yes response, it will move in a circular motion from left to right, I then ask for a no and it swings back and forwards and then I ask a better question response and it moves in a circular motion from right to left. When I say stop, it just stops still.

The Pendulum should do what you have just programmed it with, this works very well for me. Some people use back and forward for yes and round for no; it doesn't matter, so long as you know how your pendulum is responding. If you have a problem getting it to work when you first start and some do, be patient and persistent; it will happen for you.

A pendulum can also be used for personal clearing, detecting and clearing energies from your body, rooms, furniture, and property.

If you are interested in learning more, I recommend Jean Haner's book "Clear Home Clear Heart" It is a great resource to learn how to use a pendulum to clear your body. Jean teaches how to clear energy that is holding you back; she shows how to clear 'disturbing effects of others', and your inner fields, being the five ancient Chinese elements-Water, Wood, Fire, Earth, and Metal.

Each of these fields can be affected by stress and energy blockages. Each field holds different energy from anger, fear, ancestors, relationships, joy, trust, life purpose, recovering from loss to inherited issues.

Jean also teaches how to use a dowsing rod to find and track energies in homes and properties.

For many years I have cleared and tested energy in myself and others using both, a pendulum and a dowsing rod (an old wire coat hanger cut in an L shape works well). It is amazing how dowsing works.

Using a pendulum and dowsing rod is simple if you know how. I am sure you have seen or heard of people divining for water, it is the same thing.

Dowsing and using a pendulum can be fun, by using them correctly you can shift so much unwanted energy and set yourself on a path to true healing and well being wellbeing.

"The positive mind finds opportunity in everything
The negative mind finds fault in everything"

Exercises and Remedies

Daily routine to energise your mind and body 253
Healing ball exercise 265
Self-healing exercise 267
Benefits of reflexology and other energy moving techniques 268
Probable causes for common ailments 272
Life's Lessons to consider 278
Positive ways to deal with negative feelings 281
Thought-provoking questions 283
Boost your health and vitality 285
Reprogram your subconscious mind 288
Protecting and clearing yourself from unwanted energies 290
    Cutting energetic cords 293
    Cleansing prayer 295
Wheel of Life 297

Inner Smile – "Just the act of smiling changes your vibrations,
Your brainwaves, your entire body chemistry"

Daily routine to energise your mind and body

The following Daily Routine will only take you between 15 – 20 minutes once you know it. I have gathered these exercises from many different sources including, Chunyi Lin, founder of Spring Forest Qi Gong, Donna Eden of Eden Energy and many other resources that I have read, watched and learnt over many years that I have found beneficial for my own and clients wellbeing.

We are working with energy and meridians which are basic to many forms of Oriental medicine that have been used for years, along with basic moves to enhance your energy. Every uncleared emotional pain or trauma causes a disruption or block in your energy meridian system. This can lead to physical dis-ease and/or emotional pain and limitation. Since over 90% of all dis-ease is emotionally based, these exercises are amazingly effective (If done regularly) in helping treating a vast multitude of mental and physical problems.

They will help stimulate and energise your whole body and including your lymphatic, circulatory and nervous systems, your metabolism, all of your organs, your memory, eyesight, hearing plus more. They are not hard and if you think they are to start with, start slowly, do what you can, keep working on it, remember your body loves what is familiar, so make this daily routine familiar and you will reap the benefits.

It is a great way to kick start your day and even do during the day, especially if you have been sitting at a computer.

Always remember that prevention is better and easier than cure, by doing these exercises daily you will prevent many potential ailments.

So, let's get started.

1) Rub your hands together to warm up and raise energy for 5 – 10 sec's

   ➢ Place your index and middle fingers at the bottom of each side of your nose. Move them up the sides of your nose, over the bridge of your nose to your inner eyebrows and massage them clockwise five times. (This area contains many meridian points connecting to organs)

   ➢ Then continue to bring your fingers up to your forehead.

   ➢ Now place all fingers on your forehead, flatten your hands on your face and gently but firmly move them down over your temples and down to your chin.

This exercise forms a heart shape, so you are giving yourself love – Smile

   ➢ Repeat eight times

Benefits: **Your face has many energy points and nerves that connect to your brain and all of your internal organs. Massaging your face restores balance in your brain, promotes the health of your facial skin and nerves and is a simple exercise for general health.**

This picture shows the many points on your face that benefit your organs.

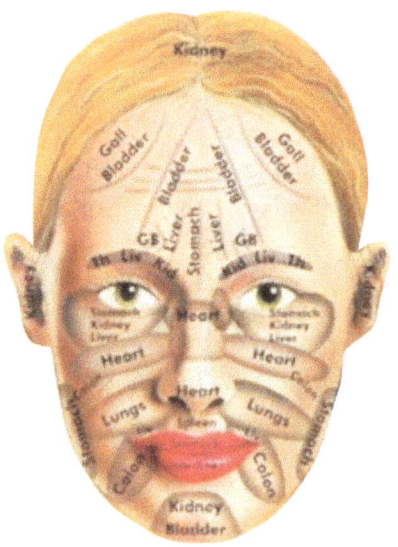

2) Make a comb with your fingers with your little fingers next to each other in the middle of your forehead and thumbs at the top of your ears, where your ear connects to your head.

Exercises and Remedies

- ➤ Comb your hair from front to back with the tips of your fingertips touching your scalp the whole time.
- ➤ Your thumbs should follow the back of your ears and little fingers the centre line of your scalp down to the base of your skull.
- ➤ Repeat eight times – keep smiling and breathe slow and deep.

Benefits: **This exercise stimulates many energy points throughout the body and scalp**

3) Cup your hands as if holding water.
- ➤ Now gently pat (cup) your head from front to back on both sides and top.
- ➤ Repeat eight times

4) Massage your ears from top to lobe, every part of them
- ➤ Now pull down on the lobe for three seconds
- ➤ Repeat eight times

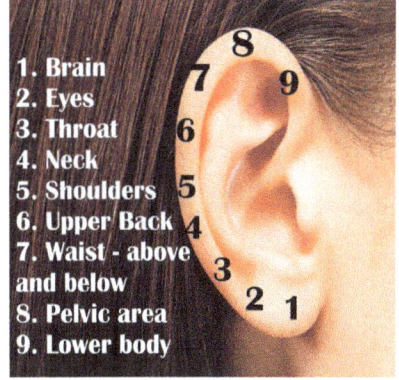

1. Brain
2. Eyes
3. Throat
4. Neck
5. Shoulders
6. Upper Back
7. Waist - above and below
8. Pelvic area
9. Lower body

Benefits: **This will stimulate and energise your whole body as your ears have acupuncture points connecting to all parts of your body. It will open blockages in your organs; it is also good for mental clarity, life force energy and hearing problems**

5) Spread your index and middle finger
- ➤ Place your middle fingers in front and your index fingers behind each ear.

- Slowly move your fingers up and down, massaging each side of your ears, 1 second up and 1 second down at least 16 times, more if you have time.
- If you have hearing problems do this several times a day.

Benefits: **This will help the circulation of energy in your ears, helping with hearing loss and ringing in your ears. Your ears have a direct connection to your brain and there are many meridian points and nerve endings on both sides of your ears which will benefit from this exercise. For example: The outer ridge of your ears is connected to your spine. The lobes are connected to your heart and liver. The inner ear to your lungs and kidneys (note, your ears are kidney shaped).**

6) Place your fore and middle fingers directly below your eyeballs on your check bone

- Massage or tap 10 – 15 sec's

Benefits: **This area of your face has 20 meridian points connected to it, therefore, enhancing much of your body.**

7) Eye exercises

- Hold your forefinger about 20 cm straight out in front of your eyes
- Keeping your head still, draw a figure eight with your finger and follow it with both eyes twice, then a figure eight back the other way twice.
- As your eyes get used to this exercise you can repeat three times (they may feel tired or sore the first time).
- Then keeping your head still look up to the right and down to the left, then up to the left and down to the right, to the

right, then left, straight up and down to the floor. Now circle your eyes slowly from right to left, then left to right.

- ➢ If you have eye problems repeat the exercise several times a day, especially if doing a lot of reading or working on a computer.

8) Tarzan Exercise

- ➢ Place your forefingers on your collarbone and move them inward towards the U-shape notch at the top of your breast bone, move them down below it and to the sides about three cm. These points are called sore spots and are often sore, this is the area where Tarzan would thump.
- ➢ Breathe slowly and deeply, in through your nose and out your mouth as you thump, tap or massage these two points.
- ➢ Tap, massage or thump for 10 – 15 seconds.
- ➢ If you wish you can cross your hands while massaging these areas, it will help release stuck energy.

Benefits: **This exercise is great for correcting your energy if it is low or blocked. It is a great energy booster, a stress reliever and helps with focusing your mind.**

9) Then move either or both hands down to the centre of your sternum to your thymus gland, tap, massage or thump with thumb and all fingers as you breathe slowly and deeply, in through your nose and out your mouth for at least 15 seconds.

Benefits: **This will help stimulate energy, boost your immune system and release stress.**

10) Arm cupping

- Extend your left arm out with palm facing up.

  Firmly cup the inside of your arm from your shoulder to hand with your right hand then down the outside of your arm to hand. Do this eight times each side of arm

- Then repeat on your right arm eight times.

Benefits: **All of your lung and heart channels are arranged on the inside of your arms; this will help stimulate energy flow and open up blockages. Cupping the inside of your arms is great if you have a cold, breathing, respiration or lung problems.**

11) Tap with both hands down the front of your body from your neck to your groin and down inner legs eight times

Benefits: **This will help stimulate your lymphatic system**

12) Cup your right hand and pat down the left side of your body from under the arm, to hip and down the side of the leg, repeat eight times.

- Then down your right side repeat eight times.

Benefits: **This area contains your pancreas channel and lymphatic system and has energy points that connect to your lungs and breasts. It will help with any problems in the pancreas, lungs, breast infections and lumps, Pneumonia and coughing. It also stimulates the lymphatic system.**

13) Interlace your fingers and massage all over your stomach and abdomen, from under breasts to pubic bone in circles either way for 10 sec's

14) Kidneys

- ➢ Hold your hands like cups, bend slightly forward, and cup or pat the kidney area of your lower back eight times.
- ➢ Turn your hands over and rub this area up and down eight times
- ➢ Turn your hands over again and with flat hands stoke downwards eight times

(If you can't reach high enough, or not sure where your kidneys are just cup as high as you can and imagine the energy going into your kidneys)

Benefits: **Your Kidney energy is your life force energy.**

15) Tailbone

- ➢ Bend slightly forward and with the back of your hands tap your tailbone and sacrum area
- ➢ At least eight times, one to three minutes is ideal.

Benefits: **Your tailbone is considered an important gateway for life force energy into your kidneys and connects to your brain and reproductive organs.**

This exercise is good for your kidneys, kidney stones, strokes, memory problems, enlarged prostate, irregular menstruation, sexual functioning problems, and constipation.

16) Hand to Hip cross over

- ➢ Cup your right hand on your left shoulder and pull down your body to your right hip
- ➢ Then cup your left hand on your right shoulder and pull down your body to your left hip

- Do this alternatively eight times

Benefits: **This exercise helps you unblock energy and will energise you.**

17) Neck

- Sit or stand up straight, keep your face pointing forward
- Move your chin to the left and around in a complete circle as if you are drawing a circle with your chin on a flat table, repeat 8 times
- Then from right to left eight times.
- Dolphin neck – With your hands supporting your back, stretch your chin forward, moving it out and down and tuck it back towards your chest. Now guide your chin up your chest until your head is back at the starting point. It is a continuous circular motion. Repeat eight times
- Dolphin Body – With your hands supporting your back bend forward stretching your chin out and forward, bend your knees, take your chin down to knees and then slowly roll up, straightening your back and legs, take head back. It is a continuous circular motion. Repeat eight times (you may wish to start with less and build on it as it becomes easier)

Benefits: **This exercise is great for stress, neck pain, dizziness and vertigo, motion sickness, headaches, and mental clarity.**

A major and wide energy channel comes up your spine and forms a narrow passage at the top of your shoulders where your neck starts.

Keeping this channel open balances energy in your neck helps relieve stress build-up, tense shoulders and blocked energy flow to your brain.

18) Bouncing

- Stand with your feet parallel and a little more than your shoulder-width apart.
- Bring your focus to your knees and bounce your body up and down bending your knees a little and keeping your feet on the ground.
- While bouncing keep your shoulders and torso relaxed and keep your spine straight but relaxed. Do this at least eight times.
- Then raise your arms straight up above your head and keep bouncing.
- Let your hands go loose, allow them to bend at the wrist and just flop up and down, do not control them. Doing this opens the channels in your body faster.

Benefits: **Bouncing grounds the energy in your lower torso helping your lymphatic and immune systems. It is also great for healing your whole spine.**

Holding your arms above your head opens the energy channels to your lungs.

There are a lot of energy channels in your wrists that connect to your lungs, reproductive organs and heart issues such as blocked arteries, blood pressure problems and recovery from heart attack or heart surgery.

19) Arm Swings

- Stand with your feet a little more than your shoulder-width apart and look straight ahead. Raise your elbows to shoulder height, keep your arms in front of you and parallel to the ground with palms facing down and fingers pointing toward each other.

- Keeping your hips stationery and head looking forward, swing your arms briskly (or slowly if incapacitated) from side to side eight times.
- Then keeping your arms in the same position, lower them to waist level and swing again eight times.
- Do several times a day if you have neck or back issues

Benefits: **Your spine is very important and has lots of energy channels and nerve systems running through it. Keeping these channels open helps keep the energy channels in your body open, enhancing energy circulation.**

It also helps with Spine degeneration, aches, and pains in your spine and Scoliosis.

20) Co-ordination and cross over

- Lift your left knee and left arm then right knee and right arm together alternatively eight times.
- Then the left knee and right arm and right knee and left arm together alternatively eight times
- Then tap the right hand on the left knee and left hand on the right knee alternatively eight times

Benefits: **This exercise helps you if overwhelmed, helps you focus and it exercises the brain. It helps with coordination and enhances your ability to learn**

21) Hips

- Find the point in your hips which is a little behind your hip bone at the same level as your pubic bone. Where you would have a dimple in your cheek ☺.
- Tuck your thumbs in and make a fist with your hands.
- With your fist tap this point on your hips with your thumb or index finger knuckle as firmly as you can without discomfort for at least 30 seconds.
- One to three minutes if you have aching hips, sciatica, numbness in your legs or neuropathy.

Benefits: **This point is a connection between the lower part of your body and your torso, keeping it open is very important, especially if your sit a lot or have any problems in the lower part of your body – hips, legs, knees.**

22) Heels

- Stand with your feet a little less than your shoulder-width apart.
- Rise onto the balls of your feet and then let your body drop back down to the ground.
- Repeat eight times or more if constipated.

    (Note if you have lower back problems or pregnant you should give this a miss, also it is not recommended to do this on a concrete floor with no shoes)

Benefits: **The vibration from this movement helps open channels in your spine, kidneys, and head. It is great for constipation, cold hands, and feet.**

23) 1000 hands

- ➢ Put your arms out to the side at waist high with palms facing upward.
- ➢ Put a smile on your face
- ➢ Close your eyes and as you take a deep breath in very slowly, raise your hands above your head. As you do this, imagine thousands of hands collecting positive healing energy.
- ➢ When your palms touch, turn your hands to face your body, start to breath out as you slowly bring your hands down the front of you, pouring the healing energy into your body.
- ➢ Then back around to stretch out at your sides and repeat as many times as you feel like.
- ➢ If you choose to, put your hands together under your chin, bend forward slightly and say Namaste, or thank you.

This is a beautiful healing exercise to finish your routine

If a mountain seems too big today then climb a hill instead.
If you're a little off colour, it's ok to stay in bed.
If the day ahead looks rough, you can always rearrange.
A day is not a lifetime, a rest is not defeat.
Don't think of it as failure, just a quiet kind retreat.
It's ok to take a moment from a stressed, frantic mind.
The world will not stop turning while you get realigned.
The mountain will still be there when you want to try again.
You can try it in your own time, just love yourself until then.

Healing ball: An exercise to shift painful energy

When doing any healing on yourself or others, always come from the heart, and send love to the area you are working with. You may need to practice this for a while, to really feel the energy flow. However, as previously said; where your thoughts go energy flows, so just know that it is happening. You need to concentrate at the same time keep a relaxed frame of mind, the less muscle tension you hold in your body and hands, the better you will do and the more beneficial it will be.

- ➢ Sit upright with your back straight, feet flat on the floor, hands on your thighs, palms facing up and you can close your eyes if you choose. I find closing my eyes allows me to focus on the energy flow better.

- ➢ Imagine loving energy coming up through the bottom of your feet from mother earth.

- ➢ As you breathe in slowly, imagine and feel it travelling up through your legs, hips, up your spine and through your abdomen at the same time, neck to the top of your head.

- ➢ Now as you start to breath out slowly, imagine loving energy coming from the universe above down through the top of your head, joining the energy from mother earth, down your neck, across your shoulders and down your arms all the way to the palms of your hands.

- ➢ Sit and feel the energy in your hands as you take a few more deep breaths and continue to run the energy from mother earth, to the top of your head, then from the universe to your hands.

- ➢ When you feel the energy, your hands may start to tingle, they may get hot. Whatever sensation you feel it will be positive energy.

- ➢ Keep breathing slowly and the energy flowing from the earth and the universe, to your hands throughout this whole exercise.
- ➢ Now lift your hands so they are facing each other and with your eyes closed imagine a ball of energy in your hands, it can be any size and colour you want, use a colour that is healing for you.
- ➢ Feeling the energy, start rolling the ball in your hands. Do this for 15 – 30 seconds, feeling the energy, you may even see the colour of it, use your imagination.
- ➢ Now place your hands on whatever area you have pain. It could be your knee, neck, head, wherever you need healing. Imagine the energy and colour pouring into your pain, dissipating the energy. Do this for at least one minute, longer if needed.
- ➢ Red is good for a knee, Green for neck. Silver is good for bones, Gold for organs, copper for nerves. Amethyst is a great overall healing colour, as is Gold. Check out the section on colour.

Pain is simply excess, unwanted energy and can be moved. If you feel it move to a different area in your body do the same exercise and imagine it moving out of your body.

"Your imagination is your preview of life's coming attractions."

'Albert stein'

Self-healing exercise:

Close your eyes and in your mind create a vortex of healing energy above your head, it can be any colour you want that is a healing colour for you. See it spinning from left to right, a cone-shaped vortex wide enough to cover the widest part of your body. The tip of the healing vortex enters the body through the top of your head, it will work like a broom, sweeping away or a blow vac blowing all toxic memories, thoughts, chemicals, substances, attachments, pain (which is just energy), anything that does not belong in or on your body.

While the healing vortex follows through with healing energy, healing and replacing all of the toxic energy that is being removed, as it travels through every organ, system, muscle, cell, every part of the body.

When it reaches your feet, you open a zip in the bottom of your feet to let the toxins pour out, down to mother earth to be processed. When you feel all toxins have left your body you zip up your feet and just feel the vortex completing its healing.

This exercise should be done slowly, feeling relaxed as you feel the toxins being swept or blown out of every cell, organ, system in your body. And then feel the healing vortex replacing old energies with vibrant new healing energy.

"If it costs you your peace, it is too expensive"

Benefits of reflexology and other energy moving techniques

Reflexology is a technique that comes from traditional Chinese medicine. It is a method of applying pressure to a range of particular points on your feet, hands and ears that correspond with all of your organs, glands, tissues and muscles in your body. This helps improve circulation of blood, oxygen and energy (Qi), around the body, relieving stress and healing pain in other parts of the body,

Reflexology can help alleviate stress and decrease anxiety. The theory behind it is that areas of the feet, hand or ears correspond to organs and systems of the body. According to theory, when pressure is applied to your feet and hands it is believed to bring relaxation and healing to the corresponding area of the body sending a calming message from the peripheral nerves in these extremities to the central nervous system, which in turn, signals the body to adjust the tension level.

There are various methods for applying pressure; the most common technique is to apply pressure with your thumbs, fingers, palms, and knuckles. Another technique is to use an object like a smooth wooden stick to apply pressure in the appropriate areas.

There are more than 7000 nerve endings in your feet alone, and by targeting these nerve endings a therapist or you, can assist the flow of energy through your body to the areas affected by illness or stress. .... Reflexology will often hurt when the congested reflex areas are treated, when sore this area needs to be worked on longer, the pain usually eases. In general, results from reflexology are often subtle and are cumulative. Therefore, you are more likely to see greater benefits from regular sessions (for example, once a week for six weeks) than if you had a session once every six months. The great thing is that you can learn how to do it yourself; there are many charts and a lot of information online.

Although reflexology is not used to diagnose or cure dis-ease, millions of people around the world use it to complement other treatments when addressing conditions like anxiety, asthma, cancer treatment, cardiovascular issues, diabetes, headaches, kidney function, PMS, and sinusitis.

With neuropathy, reflexology has a great option of gently activating the damaged nerve fibres to send and receive correct nervous signals. Through pressure techniques, a stable rhythmic stimulus of information is sent and received through the central nervous system.

It is recommended that you drink water and rest following a session as you are receiving a healing and during a healing you release toxins that need to be flushed out of your body. You may experience different reactions following a session, it is normal to have increased energy, relief from pain or other symptoms, tiredness, increased mucus, enhanced sleep, and heightened emotions.

There is no scientific evidence to prove that reflexology can cure or prevent any type of dis-ease, including cancer. However, it is still a popular form of complementary therapy for people with cancer. Some studies have looked at using it to help with symptoms such as pain, sickness and anxiety.

I have used reflexology on myself and others for many years, in particular for headaches. If you have a headache, firstly I recommend that you have a big drink of water as you will more than likely be dehydrated, then massage the ends of your big toes, they will be sore. Keep massaging and your headache will disappear as will the pain in your toe.

Reflexology is not a general massage, it is generally relaxing, however, for first-timers an authentic reflexology massage is not always going to be pleasant, it can be painful when the right buttons are pushed. If you feel acute pain at certain points when pressure is applied, this is often an indication that your corresponding organs are weak or may be having problems.

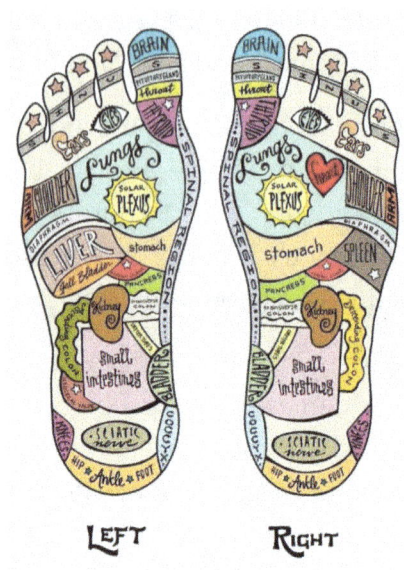

You can learn and use reflexology on yourself. It is a free do-it-yourself health regimen that you can perform at any time in the comfort of your home.

There are many charts that you can download online of the energy points to work with for the different organs and ailments.

I love working with Reflexology, Meridian points and Energy flow. Many years ago, I learnt Qigong and Qi-ssage with Spring Forest Qigong; I have also studied and practiced Donna Eden's Energy work. Many of the exercises in the daily routine use methods from both Qi Gong and Eden energy medicine, along with others I have acquired and found very beneficial.

You have meridian points all over your body that can be massaged to alleviate pain and stress in your body. It all works with the central nervous system to stimulate nerve functions helping your body increase energy levels, circulation, central nervous system, it can prevent migraines, clear urinary tract infections, help sleep disorders and depression.

With Qi-ssage we massage meridian points throughout the body, from head to toe. Qigong and Donna Eden's energy work both teach many exercises, working with energy and meridians that enhance the flow of energy and aid healing of dis ease throughout your body.

Here is one example:

If you press the "V" point at the back of your palm between the base of the thumb and the first finger this point can alleviate headaches, fevers, sore throats, laryngitis, nasal sinusitis, heart and stomach pain, eye fatigue and high blood pressure. This technique is also though to prevent apoplexy (unconsciousness from cerebral bleeding).

These techniques may be used to enhance your general wellbeing.

Refer to the recommended resources in the back of the book for websites.

If you have a healthy mind you have a healthy body
If you have a healthy body you have a healthy mind
"Life is as good as your mindset"

Probable causes for common ailments

The list below contains a few common ailments, along with probable mental thoughts, emotions, feelings and patterns that may be causing or feeding dis-ease within your mind and/or body.

To gain a better perspective, a more in depth understanding, information and solutions for these and many more ailments and physical disorders, I recommend that you purchase the following two books which I have used for many years. I have been known to call them my bibles. I have purchased many copies to give to others.

Inna Segal's 'The Secret Language of Your Body' has an extensive guide to Physical Disorders with remedies for healing and Ailments with suggested thoughts, feeling and energy they may be feeding on.

Louise Hay's 'Heal Your Body' has an extensive listing of ailments and conditions with the probable emotional causes that she felt would lead to eventual physical dysfunction.

The list below contains information from both of these books, along with other information I have used and taught from other sources.

Accidents: Inability to speak up for self; rebelling against authority; belief in violence; pain and punishment; inner conflict; feeling unbalanced; confused and unfocused.

Aches: Longing for love, to be held

Acid reflux: Difficulty digesting life; Inability to take control; feeling irritated; frustrated.

Acne: Not accepting self; feeling not good enough; unaccepted; little outbursts of anger; self-punishment; feeling not lovable.

Addictions: Looking outside of self for comfort, to ease emotional and physical pain; hiding, running away from self and others; Lack of self-esteem, self-love; self-rejection.

Alzheimer's: Suppressing emotions; hiding away from the world; loss of personal power;

Anxiety: Not trusting the flow of life; lack of confidence to change a situation; feeling helpless and insecure.

Arthritis: Holding on to toxic thoughts and emotions; feeling like a victim; unforgiving of self and others; feeling unloved; full of criticism and resentment.

Asthma: Inability to breathe, feeling smothered with love; trying too hard to please others; feeling weak, powerless, disempowered.

Back issues: Generally back and spinal issues relate to a lack of support in an area of life; holding resentment; feeling stuck; carrying burdens; low self-esteem; living in the past; different vertebrae relate to different issues, check out the charts and explanations in Louise Hay or Inna Segal's books.

Balance, Loss of: Scattered thinking, going around in circles doing too much

Bedwetting: Fear of parent / authority; loss of control

Breathing: represents the ability to take in life. **Breathing problems:** Fear, not trusting the process of life. **Lung issues:** Sad, weepy, yearning, anguished, tired and suppressed. Not feeling worthy of living life fully.

Bruises: The little bumps of Life. Self-punishment

Cancer: Feeling of grief, guilt and uncertainty eating away at self. Deep hurt, outstanding resentments. Feeling out of control with fear, anger and limitations.

Cellulite: Stored anger and self-punishment; hiding body, protection from being hurt.

Cold: To busy, too many things going on in your life; Mental confusion and disorder.

Constipation: Incomplete releasing, holding onto garbage from the past; Feeling closed off, holding back, stuck in an old way of thinking; Sometimes stinginess.

Deafness: Rejection, not liking what you are hearing; Stubbornness, isolation, don't bother me attitude; Constantly thinking or saying – I don't want to hear it; Feeling rejected and rejecting others.

Depression: Feeling overwhelmed, hopeless, disappointed and disillusioned; Anger you feel you do not have the right to have; Stuck in an old story that is only getting worse.

Diabetes: (Type 1)Longing for what might have been; No sweetness left, needing sweetness, love and care; Wanting to appear indispensable to others.

(Type 2) Fear of fully participating in life; A deep need for attention and approval.

Diarrhoea: Fear, rejection, insecure, confused, feeling helpless, lost and unsupported.

Ears: Represent the capacity to hear; **Earache**: feeling judged, not wanting to hear; too much turmoil and arguing.

Eyes: Represents the capacity to see; Inability to see ahead with joy; Conjunctivitis: Feeling irritated with what you are seeing, anger and frustration.

Heart attack: Squeezing all of the joy out of your heart in favour of money and position; Stubbornness, stress, inflexibility, a 'my way or the highway' attitude; Feeling unloved, easily hurt; holding onto guilt and regret.

Heartburn: Fear, clutching on, difficulty digesting life; Difficulty trusting and letting go

Hernia: Ruptured / abusive relationships; Feeling controlled, taken advantage of, manipulated, burdened by life; Frequent self-sabotage; Suppressing creative expression.

Hips: Fear of moving forward in major decisions; Too much responsibility, carrying others around; Nothing to move forward to.

Indigestion: Gut-level fear, dread and anxiety; Difficulty assimilating experiences, digesting life; Disappointment, fear of failure; Feeling like you are missing out on life.

Insomnia: Not trusting the process of life; Inability to relax, feeling unsafe and unable to let go; Feeling scattered, fearful, anxious and on guard.

Itching: A desire to go against the grain; Not liking what you are doing or where you are going; Irritated with a situation or person; Anger and resentment; Itching to move on, get away.

Joint Problems: Lacking flexibility and creativity; Resisting moving forward; Suppressing and pushing away hurts, sadness and frustration; Stuck in old beliefs, self-righteous, critical of self and others.

Knees: Represent pride and ego; stubborn, inflexible, won't give in; Unresolved family issues, fear of moving forward; Difficulty with dealing with people and issues from the past.

Liver: Represents pride and ego; inability to bend, irritation, anger, guilt, rage; Constant inner struggles, difficulties with making decisions; Victim, poor me, often finding fault and blaming; Can't let go or forgive; trouble sleeping and relaxing.

Pimples: Little outbursts of anger

Prostrate: Feeling inferior, stuck, sexual pressure and guilt; Rejecting, weakening your masculinity.

Shoulders: Carrying the weight of the world; holding onto too much baggage, strain, stress and worry; easily hurt; Feeling insecure, rejected, sad, distrustful; **If drooping-** lack of fun and excitement in your life.

Sinus Problems: Irritated with someone close; Frustration, fear and insecurity; Trying to keep people at a distance; Unsure how to resolve difficult situations; Difficulty standing up for self and beliefs.

Tinnitus or Ringing in Ears: Refusal to listen. Not hearing the inner voice; Stubbornness.

Remember, for more in-depth knowledge, purchase Louise Hay and Inna Segal's books.

If an issue is on the right side of the body, particularly when referring to limbs, it is generally related to a male influence in your life or your male energy. On the other hand, if you have an issue affecting your left side it is generally related to a female influence in your life or your female energy. It may be a mother, father, sibling, partner, child or a friend.

"Of all the disease, and of all the reasons for not getting well, the psychological barriers are far and away the worst"

'Dr Ulric Williams'

Life's lessons to consider

- Remember, you create your life
- When in doubt, go with your gut feeling and take small steps forward
- Life is too short to waste time and energy on hating, or putting others down
- Don't take yourself too seriously, no one else does
- Learn to agree to disagree, you don't have to win every argument
- It's ok to let others see you cry; cry if you need to but don't dwell too long
- Make peace with your past so it doesn't creep up on you; let it go
- Stop complaining, gossiping, fuelling drama, over thinking and over stressing
- Don't allow social media to control your life
- Don't compare yourself with others, we all have our own journey
- Know you don't have to please others; you are number 1. in your life
- Life is too short for pity parties. Enjoy it, start living
- When it comes to going after what you want in life and it feels right, don't take no for an answer
- Believe in yourself; know that you can do it. If you say you can, or you say you can't, you are right
- Stop snoozing your alarm it only makes you feel more tired, get up and move

- Spend more time with yourself and learn how to make the most of it
- Smile, make yourself and someone else happy, it is contagious
- Be your own cheerleader and celebrate your small victories
- Count your blessings, you will realise that life has so much to be grateful for
- Keep learning, learning something new makes you feel accomplished and keeps your brain active
- Enjoy today it is special, it is the present, the past is history and the future a mystery.
- Use your satin sheets, crystal glassware, frilly knickers, burn the candles, don't save them all for someone else to enjoy when you are gone.
- Your most important sex organ is your brain
- Always be prepared then you can go with the flow, live in the moment
- You are the only person in charge of your happiness
- Take responsibility for your actions and allow others to take responsibility for theirs. When you take responsibility for others you are taking away from them.
- Don't take things others say personally, it is only their perception and reflects their thinking. What other people think of you is none of your business
- If it won't matter in five years' time, just do it
- Know that however good or bad it appears to be, it will change. Night always turns to day, dark into light

- Forgive every one and let go, fast, don't allow them to screw up your life
- Realise that you can't change others, accept them for who they are or leave them
- Time heals everything, give time time
- Adversity makes you stronger, especially if you learn the lessons from it.
- Getting old beats the alternative, dying young
- Enjoy the sunsets and sunrises
- Never be afraid to try something new, remember amateurs built the Ark and professionals built the Titanic
- Live, Love and Laugh often. It makes life flow easier

*"People often say that motivation doesn't last,
Well, neither does bathing.
That's why we recommend it daily."*

'Zig Ziggler'

Positive ways to deal with negative feelings

- Take slow deep breaths and put a smile on your face, it activates your happy hormones
- Go for a walk, a run or do some exercises
- Spend time in nature, the beach, native bush, a park – smell the roses, listen to the birds, hug a tree and if you need an answer to something personal, ask and listen they may answer, the first thing that comes to your mind will be the answer.
- Create something – Draw, paint whatever
- Listen to music
- Meditate, Practice mindfulness
- Read a good book
- Watch a funny movie
- Call a friend and have a catch up
- Let yourself cry if you need to, let it out
- Write down all of the things you are grateful for
- Hug an animal, play with it, take it for a walk
- Do some cleaning or decluttering, it releases frustration
- Dance to your favourite music, dance as if no one is watching
- Take time to think about and understand what and why you are feeling as you are, then ask yourself if the feelings are true
- Turn your awareness to positive thoughts
- Forgive yourself if you have made a mistake
- Say sorry if you have hurt others

- If someone has hurt you forgive them and let it go
- Take a break from your phone and social media, stay away from negativity
- Do what you love doing, take a nap, relax
- Read inspiring quotes and laugh for no reason
- Repeat positive affirmations
- Write down your negative thoughts, put them on the floor and jump on them, then burn or shred them
- Pamper yourself with a bath, spa, foot soak, do your nails, makeup....
- Remind yourself that negative feelings always pass and you can change them
- Be a Self-Generating Love Machine – You are what you focus on

The Spiritual Trifecta
"Live without judgment,
Give without expecting,
and Love for no reason"

Thought provoking questions to ask yourself

- How do I respond when I don't get what I want?
- How do I deal with negative people?
- How much self-control do I have with things I know are not good for me but still tend to indulge in?
- How do I respond to situations I have no control over?
- How do I deal with change?
- How do I deal with rejection?
- How do I react when someone changes plans I have made?
- How do I deal with being misunderstood or misconceived?
- How do I deal with stressful situations?
- How do I react when put into a situation that is out of my comfort zone?
- How do I react when I make a mistake or fail at something?
- How do I deal with others mistakes or unpleasant behaviour?
- Do I follow through with promises I make?
- Do I forgive and let go if others have hurt me?
- How do I deal with the judgement of others?
- Do I accept my mistakes and apologise freely?
- How do I deal with uncertainty of the future?
- Do I look after myself, my own health and concerns?
- How do I deal with past hurts and events that have happened in my life?
- What can I give up that is not serving me?
- How do I spend my free time?

➢ Am I prepared to make changes for the better?

*"You don't have to be perfect to inspire other people.
Let them be inspired by the way you deal with your struggles,
Your heartache and your imperfections"*

Boost your health and vitality

- ✓ Drink plenty of **water** and **green tea**
- ✓ Eat a **Big** Breakfast, **average** lunch and **tiny** dinner
- ✓ Eat fruits, vegetables and **natural food**
- ✓ Go for a **walk/swim/bike** ride daily
- ✓ **Breathe** deeply– stop everything and take long deep breaths regularly
- ✓ **Read** motivational books
- ✓ Play board or card **games** with friends-It's good for the brain and social life
- ✓ **Limit** time on your phone and computer.
- ✓ Go to **bed** earlier (before 10pm) – get 8 hours quality sleep
- ✓ Stop **thinking** negative thoughts about "yourself and others"
- ✓ Don't dwell on the **past**
- ✓ Enjoy the **little things** in Life
- ✓ Quit **judging or comparing** yourself to others
- ✓ Begin yoga or **meditation**
- ✓ **Take action,** even if only small steps
- ✓ Avoid **processed** and **fast foods**
- ✓ Increase **Flexibility** – stretch daily
- ✓ Listen to **peaceful** music
- ✓ **Dance** as if no one is watching
- ✓ Live in a **tidy** Space – declutter your car, house, garage and mind
- ✓ Wear **cloths/colours** that make you feel **Happy**

- ✓ **Throw away** things you don't need
- ✓ **Laugh** plenty and give a **Smile** to everyone you see
- ✓ Share **Hugs every** day– they are free
- ✓ Get **outside** more - In the Sun, on the beach, in nature – breath fresh air
- ✓ Be **positive, kind** and **playful**
- ✓ Write **'I am Enough'** on your mirrors and read it every time you look in the mirror. And if stressed write **'I have phenomenal coping skills'**
- ✓ Write down all of the things you are **grateful** for at least once a week

Remember that all of the **effort** you are making now will pay off in the end.

The Good Life Recipe

4 Cups of Good Thoughts

3 Cups of Forgiveness

2 Cups of Kind Deeds

2 Cups of Consideration

2 Cups of Sacrifice for others

1 Cup of Well Beaten faults

Mix thoroughly: Season with Tears of joy and sorrow, along with sympathy for others.

Fold in 2 Cups of laughter, tolerance and understanding.

Stir with Love

Bake well with the heat of human kindness.

Serve with a loving smile daily.

> "Did you know, that whenever you say,
> "I think I'm onto something HUGE,
> I'm so excited,
> I love my life, I have total clarity..."
> it's like hitting an "ON" button
> that throws countless supernatural, invisible
> mechanisms into action that gradually begin physically
> rearranging the props and events of your life so
> that they'll soon yield something HUGE,
> generate excitement, inspire love, and provide clarity?
> And that whenever you say, "I don't know what to do,
> it's all so hard, I hate my life,
> I don't ever want to return to time and space..."
> it's like hitting an "OFF" button".
>
> 'A note from the universe'

Reprogram your subconscious mind, Heal your mind and body

Even though science has proved so much in the last century about neuro plasticity and how our minds work, for centuries great people have known and understood the workings of our subconscious mind.

How through amazing power of our subconscious mind, we create and heal our lives. Science is not always needed for proof; there are many stories from great people that have proven that we can heal ourselves using the power of our magnificent minds. So, you learn to use the infinite power of your subconscious mind and you too will prove it to yourself.

As I have said many times, "the words you say and the pictures you create in your mind create your reality."

If you go back to the chapters on 'Conscious v's Subconscious' & 'Your mind loves what is Familiar,' you will see how, by doing the following exercise there is a very good chance, through the words you choose and repetition, you will heal yourself.

However, as I have mentioned earlier, 'you can take a horse to water but you can't make it drink.' You have to put in the time, and believe.

The following exercise, *"Consciously Reprogramming your Subconscious Mind,"* is simply counteracting the program that is in your subconscious mind that has created your dis-ease.

Whatever your conscious mind assumes and believes to be true, your subconscious mind will accept and work on.

To relax, close your eyes and take a few deep breaths with a smile on your face.

Feeling love in your heart, believing that you can and will heal, say the following at least 4 times in a row, as often as you feel you need. (If you have a serious condition, I would recommend you do this exercise two to three times a day for several weeks, knowing and believing that your inner self, your subconscious mind, knows what caused it and how to heal it.) With repetition your subconscious mind will know what you want.

Say the following to yourself out loud (yes you can open your eyes now to read it):

"Every part of my body was created by the infinite intelligence of my subconscious mind and I know that it knows how to heal me. It formed every organ, tissue, muscle, bone and system within me. The infinite healing presence within me is transforming every part of my being making me whole and perfect now. It is taking every atom, every cell in my body back to its original DNA coding. I give thanks for the healing I know is taking place now and will continue to do so. The works of the creative intelligence within me is amazing. And so, it is."

You could try recording it on your phone and play it to yourself as you go to sleep, when you get up and if you feel like it throughout the day. The more you embed it in your mind the more powerful it will be.

> *"When you can't control what's happening,*
> *Challenge yourself to control the way you*
> *Respond to what is happening.*
> *That's where your power is"*
>
> *'Buddha'*

Protecting and clearing yourself from unwanted energies

We can attract and absorb energy from others constantly, especially in malls, supermarkets, events, hospitals, places where there are a lot of people. Energetic cords can attach to you without you even knowing it and you may start wondering why you are feeling exhausted, moody, angry or confused.

You may be a gifted person, able to feel what others are feeling. However, it can overwhelm you in crowds. There are different types of empaths, who are highly sensitive individuals, who have a keen ability to sense what people around them are thinking and feeling. Many are unaware of what is happening to them, and wondering why their energy and moods change. You are being a sponge and relieving others. You can stop it by protecting yourself.

The term *empath* describes a person that experiences a great deal of empathy, often to the point of taking on the pain of others at their own expense. If you feel you are one, you need to protect yourself before you go out, especially if you are likely to be in a crowded place.

You can protect yourself by imagining that you are putting a protective bubble or vortex around yourself, like a coat of armour so that nothing can penetrate it. You can make the bubble/vortex any colour you like, remember I said earlier that where your thoughts go energy flows, so as you are using your imagination, be creative and just know that it is happening.

For many years now, whenever I get in the car or an aeroplane, I ask my guides to protect me, to put a bubble around me, everyone else in the vehicle and the vehicle itself. I then know that I am safe.

When I work with clients, go to a meeting or any public place, I protect myself with a bubble of white light. This way I do not attract energies others are releasing, nothing can penetrate my bubble. Ok sometimes I forget, I am human, but most of the time I do it.

You can easily attract energies from members of your family and friends. If your partner comes home after a difficult day at work, has argued with colleagues or things just haven't gone right, or your kids arrive home from school angry at the teacher or some other kid that hit them, they often have unhealthy energy. They may even have attachments from others, energetic cords which they unknowingly share with you, affecting your energy.

So, not only do you need to protect yourself when going out, it is a great idea to learn how to clear yourself of attachments regularly.

When you become aware of energetic attachments, you will realise and be amazed at the effects these energies have on you and you never knew it was happening. You just put it down to being exhausted after a busy day, or think 'I am just having another bad day'.

All you need to do is use your imagination, be creative to protect yourself. Most of all, believe your powers, in yourself, believe that it is happening and it will.

You can cut these cords and clear your energy fields and I recommend you do it regularly depending on where you have been and how easily you take on other's energies. Before you do any of this work, you need to set an intention, ask the universe, your guides, your higher self, whoever you work with, to help you.

I use and teach different methods. You can practice these regularly, even several times a day if you feel it is necessary.

I have used imagination, a pendulum, crystals, and sage for many years to remove and clear unwanted energy from myself, clients and properties.

In more recent years I have learnt to clear the body of toxins using a vortex of healing energy. The following are amazing tools you can use yourself; you just need to trust, believe and use your imagination.

"If you want to find the secrets of the Universe, Think in terms of energy, frequency, and vibration".

'Nicola Tesla'

Cutting and Releasing unwanted Energy

Before you start, you need to place a bubble around yourself, to catch all of the energy you are cutting loose, so it doesn't just float around or attach to others nearby.

Imagine your hand as a sword. You can use your hand, or visualize you are using it as a sword. As I have said previously, where your thoughts go, energy flows. Be creative and just know that it is happening. If you put feeling into the process, i.e. see, feel and hear the attached energy being cut, it will be more effective. You can do this exercise as often as you need to. Clearing your energy is a great feeling.

Start by visualizing cutting unwanted energy above your head with your hand.

Then, from the top front of your head, move on over your face, down the front of your body, all the way down your legs to your feet.

Then, repeat down the back side of your head, body, all the way down to your heels.

Back up to the top Left of your head, then the right side, moving down your body, all the way down to your feet. Ensure you go over and under your arms and down your side.

Now lift your feet and cut any energetic cords under your feet.

Now imagine gathering all unwanted energy together and pushing it down to mother earth to be processed, dealt with. You could turn your hand into a vacuum cleaner, suck up the energy and then blow them down to mother earth. Once again, use your creative imagination and do what works for you.

Whenever you remove energy from your body, you need to replace it with pure white healing energy. Visualize healing energy entering your body through the top of your head, filling every cell of your body. You can use any other colour as well; whatever colours work for you.

> "Everything is energy and that's all there is to it.
> Match the frequency of the reality you want
> and you cannot help but get that reality.
> It can be no other way. This is NOT philosophy.
> This is PHYSICS"
>
> 'Albert Einstein'

Cleansing Prayer

(This is a spiritual rather than religious practice)

The following 'Cleansing Prayer' was created by Morrnah Simeona and given to the world as a gift to use freely. I came across it in Joe Vitale's book "At Zero" a book with many useful tools.

Say the following 4 times to change any situation you are uncomfortable with, filling in the dots with whatever the issue, belief, feelings, thoughts, you are concerned about, anything you want to release.

You can use the word Universe, God or whatever deity you believe in.

The Prayer

Spirit, Superconscious, please locate the origin of my feelings, thoughts of.....(Issue).....................

Take each and every level, layer, area, and aspect of my being to this origin.

Analyse it and resolve it perfectly with Universal (God's) truth.

Come through all generations of time and eternity. Healing every incident and its appendages based on the origin.

Please do it according to Universal (God's) will and until I am at the present, filled with love, light and truth. Universal (God's) peace and love, forgiveness of myself for my incorrect perceptions.

Forgiveness of every person, place, circumstances, and events which contributed to this, these feelings and thoughts.

I use this prayer frequently. I also finish with an old Hawaiian clearing saying which is said whenever anything bad happens – e.g. accident, war, bad news anywhere in the world. It is called Ho'oponopono - the 4 steps to forgiveness.

Sorry, Forgive me, Thank you, I Love You. (Can be said in any order)

To learn about and understand Ho'Oponopono, purchase Joe Vitale's books "Zero Limits" or "At Zero" or Goggle Joe.

"When one door closes, another door opens;
But we often look so long and so regretfully upon the closed door
That we do not see the ones which open for us"

'Alexandra Graham Bell'

Wheel of Life

It's time to redo your 'Wheel of Life' to see if you are better balanced after having read and, hopefully completed other exercises suggested and taken on board appropriate information and taken action to create a more vibrant, healthy mind and body.

Join the lines in each section on the 'Wheel of Life' below.

0 being not good. 10 being great.

Character — Your attractiveness, your charm or charisma

Physical — Your Fitness, level of energy and physical being

Health — Your overall health Mind, and body

Emotional — Emotional state, level of enjoyment and happiness

Relationships — Your relationships with friends family and colleagues

Career — Level of satisfaction, stimulation with your career

Spiritual — Your spiritual satisfaction, awareness and oneness

Creativity — Mental state, level of learning, mental growth

*"Dear Self: When you start taking care of yourself,
you start feeling better.
You start looking better. You start attracting better.
It all starts within you."*

Unknown Author

A Real-Life Story to Conclude with

A friend I have known for many years, Jeff Ghaemaghamy, posted an article on Facebook that I thought would be a great lesson for us all. Jeff has allowed me to use his article as he also wants to get the same message out there as me. Here is what he wrote:

"8 Years ago, today, I was discharged from hospital after suffering a heart attack... I hope my story impacts you and everyone you know.

I would like you to think deeply think about what your #1 priority in life is?

Many of you who follow me know I have been nicknamed the "Wealth Mentor" by my coach because I came from being a high school dropout $70,000 in debt and no foreseeable way to get out of the situation I was in because of poor decisions, to being in the top 1% of the population financially and living a life I love.

Today, I don't want to talk about Wealth and Financial Freedom I want to talk about the most important wealth...YOUR HEALTH!

It was 11am on December 30th 2011 and I was sitting at my computer scrolling through Facebook. I had skipped breakfast again which was normal for me and I started to feel what I thought was hunger. I popped some bread in the toaster and ate something and still felt funny it felt like indigestion which I never get. I lay down on the floor in my living room and tried to breathe it off and then felt a pain in my left arm. after a min or two, I went to my computer and googled indigestion pain in arm and up came the words "HEART ATTACK". My first thought was naaaah, I am way too young. I wasn't hugely overweight; I didn't smoke or drink. I thought I was healthy.

Donna wasn't convinced and raced me to the local medical centre. Upon arriving the pain had continued to increase and they rushed me into a room and hooked me up to an ECG, called an ambulance. 45 min later I was in theatre with half a dozen doctors and nurses working their magic.

It was surreal this kind of thing happens to other people, not to me, I am healthy. Boy was I in "denial" and I am not talking about the river in Egypt

Well here is what was really happening:

- I was eating crap food choosing fettuccine instead of fish
- I wasn't drinking enough water maybe a glass of water a day not the 6 - 8 glass I should have been.
- I was what they call skinny fat with fat building up around my organs.
- I hadn't been to see a doctor for over 20 years
- I had high cholesterol which I discovered is a combination of genetic and food-induced.
- My blood pressure was high and I was deficient in many nutrients missing because I wasn't eating a balanced diet.

Basically, I was a walking time bomb. I was in total denial and worst of all I had been teaching other people about all of the things I wasn't doing myself.

I had a very popular seminar I had delivered to over 10,000 people called "Your Health Your Decision". I wasn't walking my talk and I got a wake-up call!!!

So why am I sharing this with you??

Well, I am 100% about getting ahead financially and having a dream life financially, spiritually and being socially conscious but none of this makes any difference if you are worm food.

Even if you believe that there is another life waiting for you, it's not responsible to leave life with unfinished potential.

I believe that all of you know what you should be doing every day to live a long and healthy life...

- *Eating a balanced diet*
- *Less sugar*
- *The right fats*
- *More protein preferably plant-based*
- *Two litres of clean water*
- *Exercising moving stretching*
- *Getting seven to eight hours of quality sleep*
- *Reducing stress*
- *Supplementing to guarantee a balance of critical nutrients*
- *Thinking positive thoughts*
- *Getting regular health checks to measure blood and other areas of health*

I have a way of thinking when anything happens in life, I ask the question... What is good about this?

A Real-Life Story to Conclude with

So, I asked myself what was good about my heart attack?

- *Well it didn't kill me*
- *It was a wake-up call that evidently, I am not invincible*
- *It caused me to eat better and exercise every day*
- *It has helped me be authentic when sharing with others about the importance of dynamic health.*
- *I am more grateful for everything in my life.*
- *I finally married my best friend Donna* 🧡
- *and so much more.*

As you write down what your life will look in the next few years, decade to come I want to encourage you to make your #1 WEALTH YOUR HEALTH.

I am so grateful that today I am healthier than ever. I am exercising every day; I am eating well (most of the time) I am drinking lots of water and taking a hand full of supplements every day. I was on 7 medications and today I am 100% drug-free.

My Cholesterol and blood pressure are under control and I get my blood work done every three months. I have all of the good nutrients and trace elements I need to live to age 105 as my Norwegian great grandmother did.

Who do you know who would benefit from my story and this amazing book? I can't help but wonder if my story and others in this book could impact even just one person by starting them thinking and making changes in their life that may help them live a long and dynamic life.

Remember Prevention is better than Cure!

Conclusion

'If it is to be it is up to me.'

When you entered this world you were healthy, whole and innocent, you loved unconditionally and you knew that all of your needs would be met. Happiness and good health were your natural state of being and still can be.

Unfortunately for many, conditioning and life experiences have got in the way and side swiped them, taking them off track.

We all have our own journey and we can all be side-tracked, however I truly believe that everyone can enjoy a life of vitality, with a healthy mind and body given the will and right guidance. All you need is to be determined, persistence and have the will to want to have a healthy mind and body and to change.

As Mahatma Gandhi put it *"Be the change you want to see in the world."*

I have endeavoured to do this by walking my talk. And by sharing my many years of study and practice, knowledge and skills, offering you guidance so you too can enjoy a life of vitality and good health. And for every person I help to change, have it ripple out too many others.

Conclusion

Remember, "Life is for living. It is not a practice round, and you only get one shot at it." You can't look backwards and get ahead. Try it! Look behind you and keep on walking forwards, see what happens. Then tell yourself, "It's time to lead and not be led." Always remembering that 'Your Health is your Greatest Wealth', you can't enjoy money and possessions as well if your health and vitality are low.

Remember your attitude is your thoughts, feelings and actions all blended together and your attitude determines the altitude you soar, your standard of living.

Everyone encounters issues, trials and tribulations in life; they are all lessons to teach you, so learn from them and move on. Listen to your inner self, everything you need comes from within. Just smile, go on, and feel that essence of love and happiness deep within.

If you need an answer, close your eyes and ask the question, then wait for the answer, don't think about it, the first thing that comes to you will be the answer. Everything you need comes from within, your subconscious mind has all of the answers.

Listen to your gut, slow down, and don't be like most people who fly through life missing the clues, not seeing the signs or listening to their inner self. Your body knows, it will tell you if you are off track, it will give you a cold if you are too busy, break a bone if you need a break, give you a pimple if you have little outbursts of anger, it knows, listen to it.

Your mind and body will guide you; they won't give up on you unless you neglect them. Just like other people, if you neglect them, they will think you don't care and have given up on them. Your mind and body think and react the same, if they think you have given up on them, they will tell you by creating dis-ease within.

Remember your body does what your mind tells it and your mind does what you keep telling it, what it thinks you want. So, to me it makes good sense to tell your body what you want; stay positive feed, water and exercise it well and you will flourish, you will live a life full of vitality and good health.

You were put on this earth for a reason and life has a good reason to express itself through you. You are a beautiful soul. Know and believe it. If you find that hard to believe, go within and find your beauty, it is there. A butterfly cannot see its wings, its own beauty. When you find that wonderful person within, glow and show it to the world, share it with the world and your life will change. When you give, you receive.

I sincerely hope that your health and life have benefited from reading this book and following the suggestions within. Please read, rinse and repeat, in other words read it, take action and reread if need be, I am sure you will discover a new gem each time.

I know you are ready to take control of your life, to start living life to the fullest; actually living the life you deserve. So, determine what your values are and live by them. Be true to yourself, not to your past self, but to your future self.

The fact that this book has found its way into your life and you have read this far is more proof that you want to heal your life in some way, so good luck you can do it. You are a brilliant healer, you have more power within you than you know, and you were born to live a life of vitality, health and happiness.

I believe in you, I do, I believe that you can be the healthy person you have always dreamed of being. So be the change you want to see in the world. I am ☺

Remember there is no drug more powerful that your mind.

Conclusion

LIVE, LOVE, LAUGH AND DANCE – Life is about living, giving and receiving, having fun and being grateful for everything and everyone you have in your life.

Did I tell you that I love you? Well I do, I LOVE YOU

Aroha (Love)

It takes no energy for one flame to light another;
it costs nothing to give a smile.
Light up someone else's life, give and you will receive.

"It takes nothing from a flame to light 1000 others.
Be a FLame"

Recommended Websites and Reading

Below are the contacts for some of the amazing people I have learnt from, that have helped mould my life and in turn the lives of others around me. And now, will hopefully help you on your journey forward to a life of Vitality with a healthy mind and body. I have quoted or made reference to many of them throughout the book:

The late:

Dr Frederick Bailes author of 'Basic Principles of the Science of Mind,'

Dr Ulric Williams' 'a Surgeon turned Naturopath'

Napoleon Hill author of Think and Grow Rich

Louise Hay author of Heal Your Body, You can heal Your Life, plus many more

The very much alive:

Inna Segal author of 'The Secret Language of Your Body' https://www.innasegal.com/

John Assaraf author of 'Innercise' plus many more https://johnassaraf.com/

Joe Dispenza author of 'You are the Placebo' https://drjoedispenza.com/

Recommended Websites and Reading

Joe Vitale author of 'Zero Limits' and 'At Zero' https://joevitale.com

Anthony William author of 'Medical Medium' 'Liver Rescue' Plus more https://www.medicalmedium.com

Chunyi Lin Founder of Spring Forest Qigong – https://www.springforestqigong.com

Richard Gordon Founder of 'Quantum-Touch Healing' https://www.quantumtouch.com

Dr Daniel Amen Founder of Amen Clinics and author of 'Change Your Brain, Change Your Life' and many more http://danielamenmd.com

Dr Michael Breus, author of 'The Power of When' https://thesleepdoctor.com

Nick Orton, author of 'The Tapping Solution' https://www.thetappingsolution.com

Gary Chapman, author of 'The Five Love Languages' http://thefivelovelanguages.com

Jean Haner, author of 'Clear Home, Clear Heart' https://www.jeanhaner.com

Emily Gowor, author of 'Inspirational Bible', 'Born Great', 'The Book Within You' and many more

Jana Stanfield, Humourist, songwriter, and educator https://www.janastanfield.com/

Marisa Peer author of 'I am Enough' and 'Ultimate Confidence' Founder of 'Rapid Transformational Therapy'

Jennifer Barraclough, Author of 'Focus on Healing' www.jenniferbarraclough.com

Mark Victor Hansen Co- author of 'The One Minute Millionaire' and the 'Chicken Soup for the Soul Series'

Jack Canfield Co- author of 'Chicken Soup for the Soul Series' and 'The Key to Living the law of Attraction' Plus many more

Roger Hamilton author of 'Wink' and 'Your Life Your Legacy'

Bob Proctor author of 'It's not about the Money' and Founder of 'Life Success Consultants'

Bruce Fife author of 'Stop Alzheimer's Now'

Mike Mandel Hypnotist https://mikemandelhypnosis.com

Steve G Jones author of 'Unlimited Confidence Hypnosis' NLP Practitioner and trainer

There are many more, too many to mention, my apologies for anyone I have not mentioned, I have been learning for so many years.

Thank you to the following artists that so generously allowed me to share their masterpieces. All from https://pixabay.com

The Butterfly after every quote and the Family rainbow heart image on the relationship page were created by Gordon Johnson

All Chakras images were created by Peter Lomas

Yoga tree with silhouette Body on cover was created by Mohamed Hassan

Woman head with sayings image by John Hain

Hands and baby's feet image by Marusicova

Stressed man image by Davidqr

Heart brain health image by Elisa Riva

Image of man in the Sun by Gerd Altmann

Water drop image by Rony Michaud

Brain gym image by Tumisu

"It's not as if one could be bored enough, feel frustrated enough, or complain enough that their life would suddenly turn around. It doesn't work that way.
Whatever anyone is, they become more of and anyone can change what they become by thinking new thoughts."

Notes from 'The Universe'

About the Author

Raewyn's claim to fame is being a 'Graduate of the School of Life'.

She is so grateful to have learnt so much through life experiences, working with and studying the work of amazing people that have inspired and empowered her. But her biggest thrill is seeing the transformation within herself and all of those she has worked with over the years, by walking her talk. She has a real zest for life inspiring those around her. As she says, 'a smile and sense of humour go along way'.

Raewyn started her working life nursing and has had many different careers. She has studied and practiced personal development and several healing modalities for many years. Although a great-grandmother and retired, she still works actively as a Healer, often voluntarily, working one on one, online and running healing classes.

Her main love is inspiring and teaching people to consciously create their lives; to help and to heal themselves, hence the reason for writing this book.

About the Author

Raewyn is a life time learner, with the attitude that "when you stop learning you start dying." She is a strong believer that we do create our own lives.

She has traveled to Zimbabwe and India working in schools and shelters for homeless children and delivered motivational presentations to groups and schools.

She is the author of two biographies; the story of the life of her late sister, Janice, "Jan's Dash", and "Are there Earth Angels" the life of the late Yvonne Maber. These books were published for family and friends; however, the 'NZ Foundation for the Blind' created a talking book of Jan's Dash for their members.

"The world is a playground and life is pushing my swing".

"Natalie Kocsis'